Deeper Thoughts in the Presence of God

Volume 2

Makenneth Stoffer

Forward

Volume II of Deeper Thoughts in the Presence of God is simply a continuation of the same material being received by Makenneth Stoffer from his close friends on the Wisdom Counsel. As he receives this information through creative thoughts and transfers it to many others it is important to note a few things.

First it is important to note that these segments of information are shared in response to the desires of Makenneth Stoffer to expand his own personal awareness. The fact that we know many other souls will read these books has been taken into consideration. Because this portion of wisdom and creative thought is being laid out in front of you like a deck of cards, your creative desires many inspire you to skip around and not read this book from front cover to back cover. Unless you are inspired otherwise, we would encourage you to read the segments in order the first time, because there are some subtle transitions of personal growth that may take place. Then as you live out your life from a new perspective and return to find deeper layers of wisdom contained in this material you should open the books as guided by spirit and allow the perfect transformative thought to jump out at you, opening your mind and heart to your own path of spiritual growth. In this way we on the wisdom council and all of your personal guides can work with you on your own unique path. Believe it or not we have calculated and planned for the growth of many, therefore, when you read a phrase that speaks to you like a big slap in the face or the "Ah Ha" moment that you know is changing your life dramatically, you will know that these words were written specificity for you. We will always be with each soul that is reading this material and point out which parts were written specifically for you. Those pieces of wisdom that are found in your notes and are directly related to the activities of your life, will also be extremely personalized to your soul's growth. The true wisdom comes from your point of view as we all move through this experience together.

This is not a book that allows you to unwrap a piece of Gods wisdom and simply set it aside to consider. This book is more like a present the demands immediate attention. Consider it a present, such as your first bicycle (with training wheels of course). The wisdom counsel and your guides will be with you like parents that love you so much they can't wait to see you smiling with joy while you show off your skills at riding your new bike around the neighborhood.

The information in these books will be unraveled as you ride your new bike on a journey across town or through the mountains. This is where the true wisdom will be discovered. In the journey is where you will discover the presence of God traveling along with you. You will know that the Holy Spirit is with you when the wind is on your face and your soul is moving freely through the beautiful visions of God unfolding around you and into the future, like the people, trees and beautiful views that you have privilege to view as you pass by.

The second note that we would like to share also pertains to how this information will be received by your soul. Makenneth Stoffer, among others, has noticed that the way he receives this information is based on the emotionally charged attachments that he has to certain words and ideas from his past. For instance, the word "God" as it is used many times in this material brings forth a very personalized connection that each reader has with the most important aspect of their awareness. In other words, the way you experience this material is based on your past views of emotionally charged words and ideas. Therefore, every soul will experience this book in a very unique way as it relates to their view of what God is to them.

It is very important to note that each soul is receiving this information in a very creative and personal way. The attachments you have formed to the word "God", and many other words which you have developed in this lifetime and others, will determine your understanding of the "deeper thoughts" you are experiencing.

If you have challenges with the way in which your view of any emotionally charged word fits into your understanding of this material it is important that you either accept your view and feel confident with it or redefine it to bring about a new comfort level. A soul that does not readjust their definition of words and ideas throughout their life will feel a sense of being constricted or held back, because their view of life is changing and they must allow themselves to change with it. Changing your view of life and all of its possibilities must come from within and not be swayed by traditional views that are accepted in your local environment. The presence of God is so much bigger than your localized portion of this infinitely expanding universe.

As this material was written and conveyed to you by the wisdom counsel it was written from a certain point of view which we strongly connect with at this point in our awareness.

The word "God" from our point of view is simply defined as – **All that is known and all that will be known. God is also the one experience unfolding to express more of itself, without limitations.**

The third thing to note is that the information in these books is designed to be an exploration of your own soul, which of course is an exploration of the Holy Spirit within all. It is of the highest importance that you seek the nature of God in order to find the true essence of the Holy Spirit. As you maintain your excitement and inspiration to seek out bold new visions of what God means to you, your love for this universe will grow beyond what you presently believe is possible. This is more than just a God thing. It is a spectacular leap of faith that we are all taking together!

Definitions of words and phrases:

God ..... All that exists, and all that will exist.

God source..... Every place in the universe where God creates more of its own self through growth. The essence of creation.

Aspect of God.....Any portion of God; Souls, groups of souls, physical things, the Holy Spirit , love, etc.

Holy Spirit..... The energy vibrations that flow between all aspects of God. The spirit of love flowing like a stream.

The soul of God..... The combined working order of all aspects of God with the Holy Spirit guiding it.

Galleahbrith..... Is an ancient but widespread term for - God.

Porthole of Galleahbrith..... The birth canal of God, where soul energy transitions into the physical world.

Soul identity..... A portion of God's soul, defined by its own unique characteristics and developed from its point of view within the body of God.

Greater soul..... Your own highest expression of your soul identity. Also known as your higher self or your true identity.

Soul flame..... A portion of your greater soul burning brightly as it transitions through the porthole of Galleahbrith into the physical body. It exists for the duration of one lifetime.

Aura..... Energy vibrations given off from the burning of your soul flame. A colorful expression of the energy you are using to create the world around you.

Aura loma..... The infinite flow of all vibration which your soul flame has created in a lifetime. They exist even after a lifetime is complete, as they reunite with God source in many ways.

Point of creation..... Refers to the place where your soul flame ignites on the surface of the porthole of Galleahbrith.

Physical body..... The structure which contains and carries your soul flame from place to place in your physical world. A very dense vibrational pattern controlled by your soul.

The body of God..... All the working parts of God functioning as one.

Physical mind..... The aspect of your body that receives, translates, and transmits information from your greater mind.

Your greater mind..... An aspect of your greater soul which maintains all of your past, present, and future thoughts.

Chakras..... Energy structures of the soul flame that determine physical vibrations in your body. They are like command centers inspiring physical, mental, emotional, and spiritual activity.

Soul receiver..... The portion of the greater soul that gathers the flow of God source as thoughts and feelings.

The creator..... A portion of your greater soul where creative thoughts and feelings develop.

Soul's desire..... The portion of your greater soul where desires develop.

The mixing bowl..... A portion of your greater soul where the creator and the souls desire work as one unit to fuel the fires of your soul flame.

The resonator..... The portion of your greater soul that sends out vibrations to attract universal vibrations of the same desire. The energy attracted to these coils powers the physical creation of activities in your life.

Love..... The bond between all aspects of God and the greatest aspect of the Holy Spirit that flows like God's blood.

Streaming..... The communication flow from God source through all aspects of God to be received by your greater soul, your soul flame, your body and mind. A form of channeling ideas from a much larger portion of the source.

Light of God..... The vibrational radiance of God's love.

Manifestation..... The transfer of non-physical energy into a physical expression through the co-creative process. Making it happen or letting it unfold as desired.

Co-creation..... Creating activity or life from two or more aspects of God. God source exists in all activities, therefore, co-creation is the only form of creation.

Greater awareness..... The next larger portion of wisdom and understanding that you will allow to enter your consciousness.

This consciousness already exists; it just needs to be known from your point of view.

Simbah.... The sea of God. Also expressed as the sea of all knowing within me.

Vibrations..... The active ingredient radiating from God source, allowing things to exist in all forms.

Intention..... Plans based on your desires. A big part of your guidance system and co-creative process.

Infinite growth..... No limits on God's experience. The key reason this universe exists in its present form with unlimited potential.

Volume 2

68..... **One of the most important decisions you can make as a spiritual being while in a physical body is to develop a powerful love affair with life.** Now, each of you connected with a powerful internal feeling when the words love affair came to mind. So remember that all love affairs are powerful and unique to the individuals who are involved. In this case, the love affair is with God because life is a simple expression of god. Creating a love affair with life is the process of falling in love with the activities of God. Love affairs are always the most powerful stirrings in the deepest part of your soul. Therefore, if you are to reach the point of knowing God on this level, you must have a very strong desire to be in love with God. In this place of your soul, where love means more than life itself, is where a river of God's love pours into your soul. You should know exactly what we are speaking of if you simply remember a specific moment in your life that you felt overwhelming love for another person, place, thing, spectacular view, creative idea, or creative possibility. As you have noticed, the love can move into your awareness like a shotgun blast at any moment and can carry on for a lifetime or more. This can be frustrating at times because it is like a kid in a candy store with money in his hand. It's great while the experience is unfolding and you are 100% connected with choosing the things that will make you happy. Then you walk out of the candy store and only the memory is left but reinforced by the activity of eating your candy. The height of your love affair with the candy store experience is reached in the store then slowly fades away over time. What we are saying is that your love affairs will not last on the level you desire unless you develop and extend them. This means you must develop a pattern of loving life so much that you create a new aspect of the love affair as you walk home or go to the playground or whatever you do next. Your love affair with life is a state of mind that you create wherever you are and with whoever you are with.

God's love is within you and you are God's love. So, develop it as your desires inspire you to. God is within all of your desires. If you create the candy store experience, God is there; if you create the playground experience God is there; if you create a long meaningful hug with your mommy, God is there! God is with you in every love affair of your life. So why not make life your most exciting love affair, full of passion and dedication to God.

God is the love affair of your life, created by allowing yourself to be one with God while moving in the direction of your desires. You know that there is no difference between the desires in your soul and the desires of God. It is not possible to be in the universe and not be a part of all that God's love expresses. So live your ongoing love affair with life in the full awareness that God is expressing all of her desires through you and as you.

All of what we have said in this section can be summed up as **"life is your ongoing love affair with God."**

69..... Do not let any government, any religion, any school, any support group, any family member, or any person alive tell you the way you are going to experience the presence of God in your life. The experience of life is about you, creatively knowing God from your own desires as a perfectly healthy loving soul that knows its true path.

There is no standardized path to the experience of God. The only true path is the path that you follow. You will find your path through your music, your art, your games, your sports, your work, the books you read, the parties or social events you attend, the prayers and meditations you create, your imagination, and much, much more.

Those who support your path are the angels of your life. They support your path and you become one of the angels of their life as you return the support that they need and desire. Angels are the supporters and protectors of your desires. Angels inspire the experience of God through the process of love and support.

Assume that you are an angel to many souls, then live your life from this awareness, because it is as true as you and God know it to be. By supporting and allowing the path of others to unfold as their desires speak to them, you are allowing your own soul to grow and expand on its creative path. You will never be alone or without guidance on your path to the perfect experience in this lifetime and beyond. Don't get hung up on the rules and regulations that others project on you. Just **follow your heart and you will know God on the deepest level possible.** It is a powerful and personal experience that we are part of, yet the joyful part is sharing it with each other and being a part of one infinite experience. We are so interlocked in the oneness of the big puzzle that it is our destiny to be connected to all things at all times as we experience the uniqueness of knowing God within the creative portion that we are. So go ahead and experience God from your own point of view. It is the truest and purest way to know the deeper levels of God.

70..... Choosing the direction of your life's path is a challenging but rewarding task. It is an ongoing process that requires much attention to the details that will express your soul's desire. Your path will have many road blocks that require your decisions. These decisions are the way in which your path is defined and your experience created. Road blocks should always be viewed as if they are an opportunity and a gift from God. God's love, along with the desires of your greater soul, are the source of all road blocks. If there were no challenges in your life, your life would be extremely boring and lack direction. Road blocks and challenges always stimulate creative new paths to be opened up in order for your true desires to come forth. If you hate all of your challenges and roadblocks, you will create a pattern of hateful thoughts in your life. On the other hand, if you learn to love the challenges then you will create a pattern of looking forward to the opportunity to guide and create your path as you desire. Loving the challenges will create a strong healthy pattern for loving all things in your life. Relationships are always strengthened by those who learn to love the possibilities of personal and spiritual growth in their future. Because all we have is the future, those patterns of love that we create become a very important aspect of who we are becoming.

It is not important to know whether your road blocks are created by you, your family and friends, or from a higher power, because it is usually a combination of all of these. **There are two elements of every challenge that are always part of its creation and the solution; and that is you and God.** You and God are always a part of the new path. Every solution is reached by you being in the presence of God. Please allow God's love to flow through you in order to create the direction of your desired path.

Every time you notice a challenge developing or when it hits you like a ton of bricks, step back and speak this phrase: **What opportunities do *we* have now?** Focus on the aspect of "*we*," because you will never be alone in your decisions.

Ex.

1. *Imagine a challenge, big or small, then ask yourself the question, "what great opportunity do we have*

available now?" Then imagine how you, with the support of God, would deal with it.

2. *Repeat this process of imagining a challenge, asking the question, and imagining the solution over and over until there is no question in your mind that every challenge in your life, real or imagined, will follow this same process. When you know without a doubt that God is an inseparable part of every choice you make then you will be prepared to receive all of the challenges of life with the confidence that your path is truly following the desires of your greater soul.*

There is no reason for you to ever feel alone on your path, because you are never alone. You must know this truth and know it well. The strength which you create by knowing that God is with you will inspire incredible events in your life.

71..... If you have created a rut or feel that you are revisiting the same issues time after time, then it is time to make a decision to redirect your life path.

Obviously, you must first recognize that you are in a rut if you are going to make the decision to get out of it. **You must know that**

the best way to pop out of the rut is by looking forward to the possibilities in your future. Pursuing the path ahead of you with many possibilities will lift you out of the rut. Focus on your strongest desires not on the rut that you have created. The way out is always in front of you.

Use the technique of visiting your greater soul's awareness in order to gain the best overview. You must step into the awareness of your greater soul to discover the best path. Your greater soul can see your past, present, and future on many levels. It is a bird's eye view, yet much more complete. Your greater soul sees, feels, and knows your desired path. From the overview, you will be one with the flow of God's love in your life and all of your decisions will become clear.

Ex.

1. *Use your breath work to reach a place of peaceful contemplation.*
2. *Imagine that you are on a high cliff overlooking a beautiful valley. In the middle of this valley you see your car stuck in a muddy rut.*

3. *Notice that there are many paths from your car to beautiful villages, waterfalls, and rainbows over the hills.*

4. *Pick one of these paths that looks most interesting to you and explore it with your imagination. What do you find?*

5. *Explore as many paths as you desire, then simply laugh at the fact that your car is stuck in the mud perfectly in the middle of "the valley of opportunity."*

6. *Thank God for this powerful overview of your life and contemplate your choices.*

7. *Make a choice to leave your car behind and move on.*

8. *Imagine the path that you desire, then follow this path as a vision leading into reality.*

72..... Each soul who knows that God is in their heart in every way throughout every moment of every day are among those radiant souls that light the true path of Gods unfolding expression. Are you one of these brilliant souls, gifted in the true expression of love? Are you burning brilliantly with God's love in your soul?

A wise man knows where he has come from, where he is, and where he is going. Your soul knows these things, and knows its place in the universe. Therefore, it is easy to know the presence of God within you at all times. The future of God is certain to unfold from the love you carry within your own soul. **The greatest gift you will ever give to God is to allow God's love to flow through your soul at all times.**

You are the way, the truth, and the light of God. Share these three things freely and you will know that the eternal flame burning within your soul is God's love.

What we are doing here is asking you to move beyond faith. Even if you have never paid attention to faith in your life, it is time to move on. Faith in the presence of God is a stage within mankind that is being outgrown. It has been used like training wheels to uplift and support each soul. Faith has done its job well on this planet to increase the connection between God and man. The training wheels of faith have created a strong sense of knowing that the bike can safely be ridden, but for all of you it is time to know that we are helping you to remove the training wheels. The information era has swept over you like a tidal wave, and a big part of this information era is the direct communication you are sharing with other realms of awareness in the body of God. Many have called them the higher realms, but we would like you to know most that we are simply your extended family.

Because the tidal wave of information is changing your life so creatively, it is very important for you to allow the surge of spiritual awareness to accompany it. You are living in a new era of spiritual awareness; it is time to move into the next phase of the bike riding experience. No longer will the training wheels of faith be needed. You are now riding under your own skills.

You are now in the phase we will call "The Knowing." Faith has led you to the door of knowing, and knowing the presence of God in every moment of your life is the way in which you create a balanced, steady, smooth ride. You will feel the freedom and responsibility of this new phase as the wheels roll effortlessly over the open road ahead of you.

Whether you feel like you are ready or not, you are already in the phase of knowing. As the mind, body and soul of God expand, so do the phases of knowing the presence of God. (As God expands in awareness, so do you.) Knowing this is what creates the explosion of God consciousness that leaves no portion of God's awareness behind. Faith has kept the knowing of God's presence alive, but now God's presence is 100% alive in you, and you know it, and you know you know it. The reason we also know of it is because we have gone through this stage in our past. This phase is the great transition that many of your visionaries have spoken of as the end of times. It is the beginning of new times where the presence of God is known on all levels of awareness.

73..... In the previous section we spoke of the greatest gift. The greatest gift that you will ever give is to allow God's love to flow freely through your soul at all times. Through your greater soul, God's wisdom and love does flow, passing through to fuel your soul flame, which is that portion of you that flows out into the universe to forever define the existence of God, in its personalized form, as you. The flower of life is your soul flame burning bright in unison with every soul flame that God is. This flower radiates the love of every soul to create the reflection of God in all things.

For the brilliance of your soul flame to expand within the flower of life, you must open your greater soul to more of God's flow, and you must open the porthole of Galleabrith with your intentions to burn brighter. You must allow more love to flow through your being in order to connect with God on all levels. This magnificent process takes place when your intentions are focused on allowing God's love to flow freely through your soul at all times.

Prayer:

> Through my own choice and my powerful intentions, I allow more of God's love to flow freely throughout my being. The existence of God's love in my life is under my own control, and I now open it up to the higher realms of which I choose to be part of. I choose more of God's presence in my soul, in my life now, and for the limitless future I am expanding into. I choose God's love to be unrestricted in all that I do, say, and become.

Ex. *Sing these lines over and over as you travel to work in your car each day or before you fall asleep at night. Singing this mantra will open your soul to receiving more of God's love. I feel strong,*

I am healthy,

and I am loved.

74..... Well-being is your experience if it is your perceived experience. Happiness is your experience if it is your perceived experience. Pain or sadness is your experience if it is your perceived experience. The question is: how do you choose to perceive of your experience?

The circumstances do not provide the experience. It is your mind, emotions, and soul which provide the experience. Only after circumstances are analyzed, connected with emotionally, and felt by the soul, will they be a part of your experience. If you do not perceive it, it means nothing to your experience. Yet, even if you simply imagine the experience, that imagination brings a real experience to your body, mind, and soul. Every experience you ever have will be brought to you by your own perception. Perceiving love, creates love, therefore, perceiving pain creates pain. **Whatever you perceive, you receive.**

If you know how to control what you perceive, then you will control every aspect of what you receive and what your experience will be. The problem is that most people never question how they arrive at their perception of the experience. Instead, they just accept it as the truth because their mind has presented it as an unquestionable truth. So, how does the mind analyze its experience and take it as the truth?

We know from our interactions with others that the labeled perception of any event is extremely varied based on the workings of each mind involved. We know that some people see things that absolutely were not physically present. We know that the description of those perceived events is always based on their set of ideals and values formed by a complex network of lifelong events, most of which were never studied and analyzed because the mind presented the perceived truth as the only possibility.

So back to the question. How do we control the perception that our mind presents to us? We learn to ask for more than one view of the event or interaction. What if I saw it from that point of view over there, and what if I perceived it with the mind of that person over there, or what if my brother, my dad, my mother, or sister perceived it from here or there? The more possible perceptions you imagine the closer you are to the truth. **If you can expand your point of awareness then your perception of the event will also expand.** The more points of view that you can imagine, the closer your view will be to that of God's infinite view of the event. **The expanded viewing of any event is how we step outside of the box and redefine who we are and what the universe is.** Our pattern of past perception can be changed and improved if we simply take in more of the event through the eyes of our unified God experience. Through the eyes of God, all possibilities for your expanded awareness exist.

What we are asking you to do is to stop being just the point of God that you are and encompass the greater connection of what you truly are in that same moment. **Being you and being greater than you is not a difficult task if your soul desires it.** Your point of view combined with the greater point of view will uplift the level of vibrations you experience throughout your day. Stepping into a greater portion of God's vibration will always uplift you and your vibrations.

It is not possible to allow more of God into your awareness and not love more of the God experience. This means that **the more you learn to love yourself, the more love you will have for yourself and all aspects of God.**

So how will you choose to perceive your next experience? Will it be from one point of view? Will it be from the greater point of view, which includes much more of God in your life and in your overall awareness?

Your intuition is a big part of your greater experience. The more you expand your view by stepping outside of yourself or the box you define as yourself, the greater your intuition will become and the more productive all of your intuitive thoughts will become.

Ex. *Imagine a creative thought, idea, or interaction. Then imagine that you are a different person or that you are a larger portion of God imagining that same thought, idea or interaction from a different point of view or a greater awareness. Answer the question, how does this expanded version of awareness look, feel, and unfold?*

Try this exercise with all the people you know and all the creative thoughts, ideas, interactions, and desires you wish to explore. Expand your vision of the world and all that could be connected to it by imagining the possibilities from every point of view.

Ex. *Imagine the thought, "I love Heidi." Then imagine how Heidi's mother loves her. Then imagine how her friends love her. Imagine how God loves her. If you can feel the joy of all these beings who love her, then you will have a greater love for her.*

75..... The better you feel, the happier you feel, and the stronger you feel, the more in tune with your soul's desires you are. When you are in tune with your soul's desires you are in the flow and when you are in the flow you are in alignment with who you really are. So allow yourself to pursue the things that make you feel better and for God's sake allow yourself to pursue happiness and strength of character in all that you do.

Monitor how good you feel, how strong you feel, and how happy you are. These are the indicators of your alignment with your soul's desires. There is always room for improvement when it comes to maintaining the alignment of your soul's desires. If you give up even for a day, things can spiral away from your soul's perfect path of enlightenment.

Through monitoring your feelings of happiness and strength of character, you can notify yourself if the alignment of your soul's path feels off the mark. The quicker you realign yourself with your soul's desires the more productive and healthy your overall path in this life will be.

This pattern of realignment, once established, will carry over into the future of all your lifetimes. Believe us, it is a very good thing to be well connected with your own personal realignment process. No one is going to monitor and realign the process of discovering your own happiness on the path that your soul truly desires better than you. Yes, guidance from above will always be with you, but guidance from within is the true guidance that works in unison with all that you know, all that you are, and all that you know you are becoming.

You will never escape the responsibility of realigning your own happiness and, rightly so, you do not want to. Knowing that there is a team of willing helpers (guides and angels) strengthens and supports your soul on many levels, but it is still up to you to pursue your happiness through your soul's deepest desires.

From the source comes your desires; from the source comes your happiness, and from the source comes your experience of being loved. All things, including your desire to maintain you perfect alignment with the source, come from the source, and it's up to you to allow this connection with source to be in its state of perfection. That means monitoring and realigning with it as needed and desired.

Ex.   Memorize and use this affirmation often.

I am in perfect alignment with the source. As it grows, I will maintain my alignment and grow along with it.

76..... Have you ever wondered what would make your soul the perfect learning vessel? It is the belief of many Master Teachers that the most important aspect of a soul desiring to move swiftly towards higher levels of enlightenment is the desire to discover more by stepping outside the box over and over again. The desire to be bigger, better, and more expansive in body, mind, emotion, and soul is what drives us to discover more. The soul must want more. The soul must want and desire more than it can even imagine. Imagination is your greatest tool in stepping outside the box, but the moment you do so the box is bigger and your imagination is enclosed within your new box of awareness. **So, it is of an even higher pursuit to maintain the constant desire for what is outside of your present comprehension.**

All that has not yet flowed into your stream of consciousness through allowing more of God's love is what you must desire on the deepest level of your greater soul. You must want this on every level; the greater soul, the soul flame, the physical body and the aura which flows from you to what God is becoming. **You must desire more of you to become more of God, so God can become more of you.** The source grows throughout all aspects of you at the same time it grows as the complete awareness. The source cannot be separate from all that you are.

The desire to be more is well established in this great universe before you. So the only restriction to the desires of God are those that you create by not stepping outside the box. When the flow is 100% pure without restrictions, there is no difference between you and the source.

Ex.   *Breathe in the universal vibration of love as a long slow inhale. Allow this prana to flow through each cell of your body. Feel the universal love vibration harmonizing with every cell of your body, then as you release its full potential in your body with a long slow exhale, imagine great things awaiting you outside your present awareness. Continue to breathe in this same way until expansive universal thoughts and feelings flow into your mind and soul.*

The experience of allowing the universal love vibration to flow will synchronize every vibrational level of awareness within you.

Higher vibrations will always be created in this process. If you take this process one step further by allowing the universal love vibration to flow continually while you live your entire life, you will certainly be known as one of the great Master Teachers here on the physical plane of existence. This does not have to be your goal, but if you choose to aspire to a higher level of awareness you will certainly want to practice this breathing exercise which creates higher levels of prana within your beautiful and creative experience here at this time.

Ex.   *Another version of this exercise can be performed in the same manner with the same intentions. Simply create the addition of 2 thoughts. On the in-breath think, desire, and feel the words "Thank you God." On the out-breath think, desire, and feel the words "I love you."*

> ➤   Higher levels of enlightenment can be achieved with your desire to expand your awareness while connecting with the universal vibration of love.

77….. **Recognizing our self is the first step in the process of truly loving our self.** If we do not know who we are, how can we truly appreciate all aspects of our self? If we do not truly appreciate all aspects of our self, how can we fully love all aspects of our self? God is always in the process of recognizing and discovering all that she is becoming.

If you are to fulfill your own desires, you must recognize and truly love all aspects of who you are. When Jesus said, "The Father and I are one," he was able to say this in full awareness of its truth. He had reached the place where he absolutely knew that he was seeing, feeling, being, and knowing that God was in every aspect of everything he was experiencing. He saw himself as each and every aspect of all souls that he experienced, and in each of them there was no lack of God's full presence. He reached this elevated level of awareness by knowing the truth and fulfilling it through spiritual practice. He believed in the spiritual truth that practice makes perfect and therefore spent a lifetime of practicing in order to see through the eyes of every soul. This is how he recognized that he was, in fact, the complete experience of God. So when he spoke the words, "the Father and I are one," he knew the truth of these words in a very deep and personal way. He knew that he was a beautiful expression of the oneness at every place in which the oneness existed. In his spiritual practice, he was able to see the living presence of God from every point of view and from many aspects that were yet to be.

Ex.   *As Jesus did, look around you and consciously choose to recognize your presence within all things. To each person, place, thing, or creative idea that you see unfolding, speak the words, "The Father and I are one, and I am in all things."*

You must practice this exercise until it takes no effort to see and know yourself in all things. When this awareness flows freely and naturally from your soul, the presence of God will be known to you in its most complete form. Then you will be in the full awareness of loving thy own self as the presence of God.

If the idea of knowing the awareness in which you are truly all things is a challenge for you, then you are in great shape. The truth is this great path was meant to challenge all souls. Even the greatest of you will find many levels of love and personal growth within this grand challenge.

Just knowing of the challenge that this path provides does not make it all well and done. Imagine yourself as a mental and spiritual gymnast. You will always reach higher levels of awareness through spiritual practice, and in every stride that you make there is much more to gain. Even the gains of your greatest spiritual teachers are infinitely expanding through this process of knowing thyself as God.

With every moment you spend in the practice of shambala (that of pursuing greater awareness through placing your soul energy in direct alignment with all that you see), you will find a greater love and respect for each aspect of that which you entwine your soul energy with. The greater the entwining becomes the greater your soul becomes in the awareness of "the Father and I are one." The spiritual practice of shambala should be pursued by all. It holds us together even in the deepest darkest places of our being. As our desire for greater connectedness flows forth into the outer reaches of our being where the perceived limits of our soul are expanding into the uncharted eithers, the practice of spiritual awareness through shambala will always be one of our highest pursuits.

78..... The lessons of past lifetimes can be carried into the present experience to remind us of powerful learning experiences that have shaped our awareness of God. Our present display on the canvas of life is, of course, the image that we now see and give to the universe, but **the past has greatly defined the quality of our present moment.**

At this time, we take pride in bringing forth a lesson from the past which was created by Bonjavah. Bonjavah being the spiritual name of your present author, Makenneth Stoffer. In his Native American lifetime as a Lakota, he was known as Dewanda (the teacher of wisdom) and this is one of his most famous displays of courage and wisdom,

As a young healthy male, he displayed great skills in horsemanship. With his intuitive connection to his horses and his riding skills, he performed a rare treat for his community. In bare feet, while holding the mane of his sleek dark black horse named Bahjaywa, he rode at top speed across the ridge above his village at sun set. As he stood on the back of Bahjaywa, he signaled to his pure white horse named Shalom, who was following in the distance behind him. Shalom raced forward as Bahjaywa was slowly held back. At the point where Shalom passed Bahjaywa and the sunset displayed their silhouettes perfectly, he made the transition from the dark horse to the white horse by performing a back flip and then riding off into the sunset standing on Shalom while Bahjaywa faded back into the darkness of the hills.

When Dewanda returned to the village, he would gather around the fire with family and friends and speak of how challenging the transition from the darkness to light was and how rewarding it was after many moons of practice to be able to achieve this within his lifetime. He was, of course, speaking to the precious soul flames of every man, woman, and child within his village and beyond. The transition may look ominous but can be achieved through physical, mental, and spiritual practice. Many other words of encouragement and wisdom he spoke, but the great transition as they called it was one of his most powerful messages.

We are all members of this very special village now, and the message is still the same. In order to know a greater portion of God in your life and in your soul, you must fearlessly pursue it, by moving out of the darkness and into the light and love of God.

Ex.   *With your fingertips together and the palms of your hands aligned over the energy flowing from your heart, speak these powerful affirmative prayers. As you do so, breathe life or prana into your prayers. Breathe and speak them very slowly, then repeat them as many times as you desire.*

1. *My path is built on the spiritual practice of many lifetimes, and I will not stray because the presence of God is found within my life each day.*

2. *The vibrations of my new awareness are now resonating on a higher level. From this higher place I know God to be one with my soul. In this love, I shall always be.*

79….. In any one moment of your life, there are things happening to you, through you, for you, because of you, and as you. In the process of being alive within the body of God, things happen.

The fact that things happen is a direct result of our existence as the expression of God. **Be thankful that things happen and we exist.** If they did not happen, we would not exist.

Within your own experience, you may choose to perceive what is happening in many different ways. If you choose the perception **"it is happening to me,"** then you have the option to view it as good, bad, or indifferent. There is an infinite range of choices in your perception. Anywhere from "I am a victim" to "I am a victor." You may even choose to be aware of the victim and the victor in the same moment of perception. The key is that you creatively choose your own perception. In truth, you are experiencing all perceptions at once because this is the full awareness of God, which you are never separate from.

If you choose to experience more of what is happening through the perception of **"it is happening through me,"** then you will find a perspective that is more expansive and free flowing. If you choose to experience more of what is happening from the perception of **"it is happening because of me,"** then you will find yourself on the powerful path of responsibility. If you choose to perceive more of what is happening from the perception that **"it is happening as me,"** you will be opening your awareness to the greater presence of God on many levels. You will be connecting with the partnership of all things working their magic within one perfect flow of our being.

The truth is all perceptions are taking place at all times in the body and soul of God. All perspectives are very important because God does exist as all perspectives.

Do not diminish your unique combination of perspectives. When God chooses to experience life as you, your choice of perception becomes a co-creative process. Your choice and God's choice become one. As God, what do you choose to perceive? What levels of love do you choose to perceive now?

80..... **The greatest thinkers of all times are those who open their minds to the greater presence of God so that wisdom beyond the capabilities of their own mind can be accessed!** Surpassing the capabilities of one mind is not a rarity in this universe. In fact, it is one of the most important and well used techniques to raise the vibrations and awareness of all aspects of God. Most souls are aware of when their thoughts and emotions are greater than they have ever dreamed possible.

"Inspiration from above" is a phrase you have heard many times from artists, musicians, spiritual teachers, speakers, and leaders of large or small movements that change our world. Teachers, scientists, inventors, and many more will tell you that the gift of their creative new awareness has come from above.

This should be of no great surprise to even the simplest minds because the inspiration from above will never restrict itself to the workings of any mind, simple or complex in nature. It is seen throughout your planet, even in the intelligence of a simple vine reaching for more light through its desire and love of life.

It is important that you expect to think and feel greater thoughts throughout your life and within your greater soul. Expecting it will make it so.

To think and feel the presence of God from beyond the awareness of your present soul is your spiritual birth right. As you choose to open your mind to larger aspects of God's growth within you, so shall it be. Remember that your mind will receive greater things than you ever imagined possible, and you should live your life in accordance to this powerful truth. **Be ready and willing to respond to the presence of God on a much greater level every moment of your life.**

81..... For what reason do we enter the physical body and physical world? Do we really need or want to be here?

There are so many reasons that we enter a physical body that it would be impossible to list them all and how they relate to the personal desires of each soul. For your own personal soul flame, each lifetime has many different components. Most of these are of your own choosing from the desires of your Greater soul, but many more components are also of your own choosing from a place that comes from all souls. This would include the desires of all groups of souls which function as a greater unit. Examples of this would be "The Wisdom Council," "The Congregation," and multitudes of gatherings throughout the universe that define different aspects of God. The largest aspect of you which has chosen to manifest here, of course, is the complete presence of God. So, on all levels you have chosen to be here and chosen to create all that you can in the time you have allotted for this portion of your soul flame experience. **You have designed and created this physical experience from every aspect of your infinite being. So yes, you do desire and want to be here!**

Your soul flame is here to burn brightly with the fuel of God's infinite source. Imagine an infinite flow of light continuously expanding. This is God and this is you, growing like an infinite flower in bloom. Your love and your light are unfolding in every moment and in every direction.

Among the major reasons your soul flame is burning brightly here and now, while unfolding into a much greater aspect of the infinite flower of light are: expansion of love within your greater soul; expansion of your awareness; to experience happiness and joy on all levels; to fill the cup of gratitude and consume its wonderful blessing; to know thyself; to be one with all that you are; to cherish the shared experience; to greatly enhance your connection to all things and all ideas; to allow creativity to flow endlessly from your soul; to be an anchoring point of light that supports all aspects of God.

Ex.

1. *List all the aspects of why you have chosen to be here on the larger scale of things and from the powerful point of view that is of your own personal desires.*

2. *Read over each aspect of why you have chosen to be here and spend a few minutes feeling the emotions that stir within you. Feel your connections to the reasons you are here and notice that they are the strongest vibrations in your soul.*

3. *Answer the question, do I really need, want, and desire to be here in this present moment and write a paragraph about why?*

4. *Sign and save this document; it is a sacred covenant with God that you will honor from the depth of your soul.*

82..... Over the years of human existence on planet earth, many have wondered about their transition to and from this place. The entry and exit to and from this place is the same throughout the physical universe. A portion of your greater soul is allowed to flow through the porthole of Galleabrith in order to radiate as a uniquely powerful soul flame that functions in cooperation with your physical body. This soul flame experience is always connected to the greater soul and the source of God in order to do its work, play, and creatively explore in the physical world.

The porthole of Galleabrith can also be referred to as the porthole of God. It is that tunnel which your soul flows through when you enter at birth and exit at death. It is also used as a conduit for all spiritual awareness flowing from the source to your greater soul, to your soul flame, to your physical manifestation and back again. It is a conduit that holds your personal identity intact while transferring the experience of your life to and from your greater soul. Without this connection, your personal identity would flow into the all-ness without definition or direction.

Your energy signature or soul identity is very important because it helps to define unique aspects of God which can then interact with each other. This allows much more activity to take place within the body of God. **There will always be an aspect of your love that flows endlessly in all directions without definition, and**

43

it does support all activities within the awareness of God. However, the signature that your soul creates is where the majority of Gods focused activity takes place.

As the spiritual vibrations of your soul flow through the porthole of Galleabrith, you are known as God and God is known as you. This is where the expression of life takes place through you to create more of God. Spiritual interactions and the activity of life are produced from this unique form of playful awakening. It is the place where God becomes all that God chooses to be.

Imagination, focus, and intensions play a very big role in this process of Co-creation. Being thankful and grateful for the beautiful definition of God that you are is of highest importance in the creatively expanding awareness of God. When you transition into the world through the porthole of Galleabrith, your life is created and when you transition back through the porthole, your greater soul is nourished with the memories of your lifetime.

83..... The more we listen to our thoughts and connect with our feelings the better our connection to source is. Listening to our thoughts is how we channel all of our mental activity from the vast source of God. In listening to our thoughts, our Master

Teachers in counsel with our greater soul will come through as the thoughts, feelings, and voice of God.

Everything we do is the channeling of God source because that is what we are. It is simply a matter of clarity when it comes to how well we connect with the deepest desires of God. When you begin to see the beauty within all things, your clarity is reaching its highest levels. At this time, you will naturally and easily act in accordance with the beauty in every interaction of this grand experience called life.

If you see it, then God sees it. God sees it through your eyes, and it has been made to be yours. Thus, the power of God is yours, made evident by the beauty that you see and the love that you express.

Ex.

1. *Stare at something or someone until you see the beauty of its outward appearance.*
2. *Stare at it until you see the perfection of its natural organization.*
3. *Stare at it until you see the infinite beauty.*

4. *Stare at it until you see the beauty of God radiating from it.*

5. *Catalog this beauty in your memory and put it in a very accessible place within your mental and emotional being.*

6. *Choose to remember its beauty for all of eternity.*

7. *Know that you have experienced God's beauty through your eyes and that it is always accessible in this form.*

When you can perform this exercise for everything from your loving mate to the dirty pile of clothes in your room, you will start to understand the wisdom in God's love for all things. **When you connect with God's beauty, you connect with God source.** Whether it be through thoughts, feelings, or actions, you must connect with them and become them.

84..... Do you remember your early childhood and the process of learning to respond to your surroundings? Do you remember learning to love, to communicate, to eat, to crawl, to walk, to speak, to walk and speak at the same time? Do you remember learning to read, write, use tools, and operate vehicles? All of these things are fantastic achievements. All of which support each other in a never ending process of personal growth. God knows this is an unbelievable process that proceeds many greater things to come.

The question is, how do we respond to our surroundings? It can be answered simply by stating that we are the flow of God from a personal point of view with the desire to know and love our self more deeply. Therefore, we are in a constant state of connecting with our self as God, so we respond to what we desire to become, and we accept it perfectly by being in the flow.

You start to recognize that the process of growth (being and becoming) works most efficiently as you allow the energy to flow freely. It expresses as trial, outcome, and retrial with calculated adjustments. The process is monitored and adjusted by you, but always fueled by God's desire to know and love thyself.

The way in which we control our process of personal growth is so simple it hardly needs mentioning because we do it so naturally. But we do need to be reminded of it if we are to process and view it from a greater perspective. The process can be stated in many ways, but one of the simplest to understand is – **we move toward the things that we desire, and we move away from the things**

that do not serve our needs of becoming greater than what we are in this moment.

Ex.

1. *Repeat this mantra: (Good thoughts in, bad thoughts out) or (good feelings in, bad feelings out).*

2. *Contemplate how important it is to live this process.*

3. *Repeat step one and two again and again if you desire to strengthen it within your mind.*

4. *Repeat the following mantra while thinking the words of the first mantra.*

   "Oh yeah ohm (Good thought in) – Bah yeah oh (bad thoughts out)"

   ➤ *Connecting ancient words with the meaning of your present day words will help you connect with the core of your soul which spans over many lifetimes.*

5. *Then move on to repeating only "Oh yeah ohm" while thinking "good thoughts in."*

   ➤ *The focus on "good things in" will automatically push the bad thoughts out, especially, if you open your arms and heart to receive the Holy Spirit while performing this exercise.*

6. *Repeat "Oh yeah ohm" in your mind and throughout your day to enhance your growth and abundance.*

7. *Convince others it will make them feel good if they do it with you. Then good things will flow into everyone and everything around you.*

85..... Being alive means that you are engaging in the movement of energy. Self-initiated and self-guided energy movement equals life. Rocks falling, wind blowing, ice freezing, and waves splashing are energy movement that greatly effect the planet, but are not alive because they do not self-initiate energy movement. All things that initiate energy movement are alive and self-aware to some degree. Therefore, they should be treated with great respect because it is no small task to co-create life in this way. When was the last time you asked yourself to recognize and respect all of the living things around you, including the spiritual realm? If you can not recognize and respect life around you, how are you going to manage your own personal life energy as it is forced to interact with other life forces? Even the consumption of other life forces demand that you recognize and respect the energy that you are interacting with. If you do not recognize and respect a poisonous plant or toxic animal then your life can be altered permanently.

Connecting, sharing, communicating, organizing, and focusing are the things that help create your life on a physical and non-physical level. Therefore, these are things that must be understood on higher levels in order to continue your growth and move on. Recognizing and respecting all energy movement is very important to you and your understanding of the co-creative life force of God.

Respecting all forms of life is the first step in understanding your own life. It's interesting that you are so complex in your life form, yet you have forgotten many aspects of how you got to this point. This means that some of the respect you have for your own life form has been lost or taken for granted. You must regain your respect for all life forms including your own every day that you wish to expand your personal growth. **You must stay connected with the life force of God throughout every moment of your awareness.**

Ex.

1. *Look around you and stare at something that is alive until you feel its presence become one with yours.*

2. *Do this as many times as you choose with the living things around you until you feel the presence of God flowing between you and all the things that are around you.*

3. *Feel the connection between all things and feel the wonderful presence of God in all aspects of the life energy around you because it's all part of you.*

How has this exercise changed the level of vibration in your own soul? If your soul energy has raised to a comfortable new level, then you must share it with your surroundings.

At any point in your life where you wish to experience and express more life within your soul, simply use this exercise to inspire it. Life is a flow of energy in all directions - harness it and ride off in the direction that your soul desires.

By opening a channel between you and something that is alive, you create a vessel which will always be filled to overflowing with God's powerful loving energy. God's love flows automatically into all vessels that are created from the connection between living things. When you raise the energy vibrations around you, great things will happen, and that is the way it is supposed to be (by God's design.)

86..... What is the most important aspect of accomplishing any growth experience on the physical plane of existence? It is very simply the ability to connect with your greater soul so that the flow of God can be used to expand your awareness. You must get in touch with the energy that your greater soul is allowing to flow through your soul flame. Opening your heart, your mind, and your physical body to the flow of your greater soul is done by attracting the highest state of awareness to all that you are doing. Allowing your brain and body to be relaxed, confident, and in the highest state of vibration is the key to allowing your energy to be in the flow of God.

Meditation, prayer, and positive thinking are all good ways to open up to the flow, but the simplest way to allow more flow is to breathe in and then release all tension that is standing in your way. **A breath and the desire to be in the flow is all you need.**

Every breath brings in new life and prana flows. Breathing connects quickly and efficiently to all energy in your system. Even the person that is about to jump out of a plane and sky dive for the very first time must connect with his breath. If he doesn't breathe before he jumps, he certainly will after he jumps when all his vibrations are heightened by his intention to live and expand his awareness through this intense experience. When you have the intention to live, prana flows easily.

So, relax, breathe, and allow your desires to live, to flow directly from the source!

Ex.

1. *Take in a long slow deep breath.*
2. *Release the breath slowly while thinking or whispering the phrase, (relax, release, and let my desires flow.)*
3. *Allow your breath and this statement to be repeated for a powerful 20 minute meditation.*

87..... Everything in your life is about what you desire. **Your future is all that you have, and the only way to create your future is to construct it out of the building blocks of your desires.** What you do not want in your future means almost nothing. In fact, the blocks that you try to create from what you do not want will never be useful. They will take up space and only serves to trip you up. The building blocks of your life must be built out of true desires that you need and can use right here and now.

All of the universe works by creating what it needs. The stuff that it does not need is automatically set aside when it decides what it needs.

If you find yourself defining what is not needed in your life, then you must quickly turn your thoughts into what you do need. Every moment you waste with what you do not need is time that could have been very productive in pursuing what you do need. To function on the highest level, you must become a needy person. Not in the sense that you need things out of lack, but in the reality that you need things to expand who and what you are for the good of all. Love is based on need and, yes, we all need it in all forms. We need it as a part of everything we do. Growth can only take place through the need for it. Accomplishment is created through our needs. It's all created from our desires and what we need in order to learn and grow.

The sooner you can let go of the attachments you have to what you do not want, the sooner you will release your fears and move on to create the true desires that you have in your heart and soul. Your desires are from God, as all things are, so allow your desires to blossom into what you need in order to express God as you.

Ex.

1. *Make a list of all the big things you need in life right now.*

2. *List all of the small things that you need in your life.*

3. *Study these lists each day and pursue them. Like a prescription, these things you need for your life are written in front of you now, and you have no excuse not to fulfill them.*

4. ***Write the prescription and fulfill it.*** *Follow this process and teach others to do the same.*

This is your life; only you and God know what you need. Go forth and create what you need by following your soul's desires. **Be sure of what you need by asking for God's love to guide you, as it always has and always will.**

88..... Decisions based on "knowing the desired result," are your strongest decisions. Builders, designers, inventors, and engineers absolutely must know what the desired result is if they are going to be successful at constructing a building, road, bridge, boat, vehicle, etc. They must know it to a point of perfection if the customer is going to pay them for it. If it's not perfect, they redo it until it is perfect.

Builders draw designs while imagining building and completing the project many times over before it is started in order to confidently know the desired result. They use personal and past experience to support their beliefs in the final product, and they know their skills very well, including their limitations.

If every person would follow this process of knowing their desired result on each of life's projects then they would achieve the results they desire. When you decide to build a new part of your life or a new path to follow, you must do what it takes to know the desired result, and then pursue the creation of it.

Ex.

> *Pick a spiritual goal for your future then follow these four steps. After each step ask yourself how well do I know my*

desired result, how much do I need it, and what is the

effort required?

1. *You must imagine it.*

2. *You must build it in your mind.*

3. *You must lay out the details on paper.*

4. *You must follow the steps that take you there.*

Now explore other goals in your life the same way.

When you know what you want to create and you have a plan to do so, there is nothing that can hold you back if your desires are strong enough to see it through. Even road blocks will not be able to hold you back. <u>There is no road block strong enough to hold back the desires of God.</u>

89..... Many wise individuals have proclaimed that **you must be willing to fail in order to succeed.** This statement is very true, but it can also be said that **you must be willing to move forward in order to succeed**. Moving forward is what we do. Failure and success are only terms used to describe your feelings of where you are at. Failure and success are only temporary descriptions of your point of view at a certain place in time. That point of view is only one of the many powerful points of view taken by the presence of God from infinite locations.

The element that ties all viewpoints together is that you are willing to move forward. **When you proceed forward with your intentions, you will always be adding something new to your awareness and the growth of this universe. Everything that has conscious awareness is in a perpetual state of moving forward.** When you recognize the truth of this simple reality and choose not to suppress it with fear, your life will be limitless.

You must remember that growth is always unrestricted. Proceeding forward with growth is the nature of God. It is and always will be your path. The wisest of you will know that success is the most appropriate term to use in every step that you take. In the end, which is always the beginning of something new, success is the only true reality.

Perfection is not a stopping point; it is a continuous process of you expressing your divinity in the complete presence of God.

Ex.

Memorize one or both of these statements by repeating it over and over until it settles deep in your soul.

"I proceed forward with success because it is what I do."

"I am willing to move forward in order to succeed."

90….. Human beings were designed as biological problem solving machines. Everything we do is in some way designed to overcome the challenges of life. **Growth is challenge unraveled and reorganized.** You will always be challenged and you will always be in response to your challenges. You will always be charting your new destiny, in your mind, your soul, your emotions, and your physical environment.

What makes your path diverse and totally unique is the steady flow of challenges. As you swim through them at the pace you desire, each road block gives you the opportunity to move creatively in a chosen direction. This forces you to choose a problem solving technique in order to move on. Rarely do you blast through the problem simply to maintain the same path you were on. When you encounter each roadblock in life, you normally engage it with great enthusiasm on a deep soul level because of the excitement in the challenge. Your mind and emotions might be "freaked out" by it, but your soul is always ready to create the exciting new road ahead.

Imagine that you are standing in front of a beautiful gate and a playground/amusement park/circus of fantastic proportion is happening in front of you. It is so vast and beautiful that it is mind boggling. Then the gate attendant asks if you would like to wait for your mommy to pay your way in or just climb over the gate. It doesn't matter to him; he's just there to do his job, which is to remind you that you can choose any direction in which to go. As you enter and choose a direction the attendant yells out "this is your life, have fun, and don't forget to ride the rollercoaster because it is one of God's masterpieces. You can see everything from the top of the first hill, and if you ride fearlessly, with arms in the air, you get a free prize at the end."

Now does this scenario enhance your enthusiasm about life's fantastic road ahead? Do we as your guides and angels need to push you through the gates to your next great adventure? Most of you race off so fast that we can barely keep up with you, especially those of you who really love life's rollercoasters. **Remember everything in life is just one decision away** unless it is one of those special things that takes many decisions in a certain direction to actually discover that there is a massive life changing decision ahead of you. Either way, **there is always a roadblock, a**

decision, and a path to follow. That's just the way it is. This is the process that expands the consciousness of God into all corners of the universe in order to experience all things. Remember these words at each roadblock: **Thank you God for this opportunity; let's go play.**

91..... What are you hanging on to? **The only things that you should be hanging onto are the things that you are willing to let go of at any chosen moment.** In fact, it will set your soul free if you simply learn to hold things gently and then set them aside to experience the greater things in front of you. Even love should be held ever so gently and expanded upon. The powerful and expanded awareness you are extracting from these writings are simply a place on your path, a place to rest and take in the enormous view of your future path into the vast awareness of God. **With each gem that you find, tuck it away and move on.**

You never lose things because they are always held in your memory. Yes, the future is built on the strength of your memories but only if you allow them to transform into something greater. Your life and your soul expansion is like a flower that is forever continuing to expand its blossom, a few peddles at a time. So don't hang onto anything for too long so that you can allow the beauty of your soul to be surpassed each day. **Allow your soul to be born again in the beauty of God's new love.** Hold all things gently and then set them free.

92..... How often do you stop to review the activities of your life? This in an important process, that is used in order to update your mind on the true path that you are following. Because you are constantly growing, your old methods of being and doing just don't serve the needs of your new awareness. Some people call this the process of maturity and believe they understand it enough to predict the future of change in the souls of their friends and loved ones. To some degree, this is true because there are some growth patterns that are used by many. But, your soul is much too creative for anyone other than the owner and controller of it to analyze and project the course of your own life.

No one other than yourself should attempt to review and analyze life while not being in the controller's seat with the ability to direct the course of your life in accordance with your soul's desires. It is up to you to review your path and change it as you know best.

Please do not hesitate to change your life because you will always know what is best for your future based on the things your soul knows it needs from this truly unique experience. We know that this reviewing process happens many thousands of times in each person's life because we are right here with you watching from a higher perspective. Many times a road block will initiate the mind's review process in order to solve a challenge. Sometimes the road block is so big that it inspires a review of your complete life. Ask anyone who has had a near death experience if a complete review of their life took place in a matter of timeless moments. This review process is hardwired into your brain with its connection to your greater soul.

We all know how important life reviews are, so why don't we consciously think about the need to review our life, and then become more actively engaged in reviewing it, along with projecting our needs to acquire the experiences that our soul desires? We must review the past in order to preview our future.

You have become a soul with much higher awareness, evident by the fact that you are reading and contemplating deeper thoughts in the presence of God. With this being said, we would like to suggest that you make it a productive habit to review and project your life path forward. Start by reviewing the events of the last few minutes or hours of your life. Is anything there worth analyzing, understanding, and projecting into the future? Then review the last day or two, last week, last month, last year, etc., etc. If necessary, review relevant portions of past lifetimes. It's all in there, and if it's needed it will flow out as you allow it.

If your intention is to direct your future, then you will be much more affective when your conscious mind is in alignment with your soul's desire to review and project your life path forward. You must remember that reviewing your path is very important but is a small portion of your life. When exploring the wilderness or exploring a cave, you must look back and remember the way you have come or you will become lost. Don't lose your way, moreover, review the details of your past so you know where you are going. Less than two percent of your life should be spent in reviewing and ninety-eight percent should be in traveling the path ahead of you. The path in front of you is everything; yet, its meaning could be lost without the path behind you.

93..... How does a genius create himself? We all have the stuff that makes up a genius deep within us. So why do some people hold it back to the point where it is not being used or even recognized? Fear is the main culprit in subduing the genius, while personal growth is the way to unleash the genius within you.

A genius creates himself by asking questions and searching for new meaning in everything he does. A child is a brilliant soul that questions everything in order to learn amazing things very quickly. In the early years, a child is always a genius because they question everything. So, that is the answer; just be childlike and ask every creative question that you can and the genius will arise! That is why we have provided so many questions in this book; because there are so many geniuses among you, and we wish to inspire you to do the same.

Fear not the answer. You must ask the question in order to discover the truth!

Every aspect of your physical emotional, spiritual and intellectual growth depends on the amount of questions that you ask in order to pursue a healthy growth experience. Most of these questions are asked in your own mind and answered in the presence of God. The genius gathers much information from God because God is the source of all information. If you are not asking questions or inquiring about the nature of things, then you are holding back your true genius, not only in your life but for the benefit of the universe and all that God desires to be through you.

Ex.

> *Try taking one whole day to step outside of every situation and ask questions about everything you see taking place. Search, seek, and explore the known and the unknown like a child would. Make the decision to continue it for another day and so on. At some point, each and every day will be filled with powerful learning experiences created by your inspiring questions, and you will know first-hand the wisdom of becoming the genius.*

94..... Most human beings look at their life as a continuous array of ups and downs. Because your greater soul looks at it in a slightly different way, we would like you to consider adopting the view of your greater soul. The way that God, your greater soul, and all of your angels and guides look at your life is that life is a series of opportunities for spiritual growth.

The further away from your greatest desires you are, the greater the opportunity for dramatic and exciting change. The opportunity for change is one of the main reasons you exist as a soul flame in the physical world on the planet that you now inhabit. **The availability of opportunities in the physical universe are much more accessible and dramatic than anywhere else in the known universe.** If you desire a powerful spiritual experience, you come to the physical plane of existence, and that is where you are at my friend.

If you make it a point to embrace the reality that life is a precious opportunity, then you will be much more in tune with your greater soul and the presence of God. Your path will be filled with much greater reward than you ever believed possible. Pursuing healthy change through opportunity is your true soul's desire. You must know this and know it well.

Ex. Memorize and speak these words often:

> *"All activities in my life are opportunities leading to greater opportunities."*

95..... There is much to be said about simply being and knowing that you are in the presence of God. There is also much to be said about learning and becoming. Learning and becoming will allow you to reach a greater awareness of being knowing, and vise-versa. Daily meditation will keep you in the flow of being and knowing as you pursue this practice.

Learning and becoming will also be up to you and the desires of your greater soul. The first choice you will need to make is to hold strong to your intentions to learn. This involves the decision to "learn to learn".

Learning is an ongoing process with the first step being 'Learning to Learn". Start by clearing away all preconceived ideas. Find that state of being where you release all things and all ideas. Then allow the most important challenge of your life to step forward. Life is very much like the game of Go. If you can define the biggest move on the board at any time, you will be making the move that creates the greatest gain. Right now your biggest move is to learn how to learn.

So you must search for your greatest challenge. What you define as your biggest problem will give insight into your greatest challenge. It will not always be obvious, so you must explore, define, and redefine what you believe is your greatest problem at this time. The path between where you are and where you desire to be is the challenge you seek. If you see great potential for growth, it is likely the challenge that you should pursue. Then you must tune into your desires and the presence of God that will support you through the learning process.

It is always a good idea to ask for and pray for guidance in understanding the appropriate move that you should make on the board of life. Then, step back and view your choices from a place outside of yourself. View the bigger perspective of all choices. **View it from all possible perspectives, then choose the path that your greater soul desires in order to solve the challenge.** From this process you will always make the appropriate choice. Even if it looks like a possible sidetrack, remember that there are many stepping stones on the path to solving all of your greatest challenges. Again, remember that solving a challenge or set of challenges is an ongoing process of learning, which involves the elimination of the choices which do not solve the challenge in the way your soul desires. Try something new; try something different to find your way. Remember that every trial path redefines the challenge and the new path. Learning begets learning, and your effort must be continuous.

Try, try, and try again, this is the ultimate learning process. The rewards are great and even greater after a long road travelled.

Your present level of learning will always be enhanced by greater levels of learning, even from one lifetime to the next.

Those of you that learn to enjoy the process of learning and becoming will always get the most out of your lives. So, never separate from happiness in your process of learning and becoming. **Get excited about learning and stay excited because it is a long fulfilling process, and it defines what you are becoming.**

As you follow in the wisdom of those who have gone before you, you shall be happy to know that not all of your efforts to learn, grow, and expand your awareness are based on simple trial and error. A great foundation has already been laid to support the creative new paths that you soul desires. The path ahead of you is clear and sunny, and God will always be with you.

96..... Every soul existing offers bundles of vibrational energy at each moment. These vibrational offerings are what your soul is creating here. **All beings create their reality by the vibrational energy which they offer to the whole experience of God.** The whole vibrational experience of God, in turn, responds to every existing energy vibration with all of their unique identities and all of their creative agendas. The sum of this interaction we have discussed many times, is the co-creation process, which simply means that each individual soul works in unison with the whole to create all aspects of God's ongoing experience.

Because you are a very intelligent aspect of God, it is important to discuss the way in which a soul of your intelligence creates and consciously controls your experience. Consciously controlling your experience is the desire of God that is flowing through you now and always. Everything that lives consciously controls its experience to the degree that it connects with the process of co-creation. Because you are ready and know that you are ready, we have chosen to help you expand your awareness of this process. This will help you step into a much greater portion of the light as you so desire.

Co-creation of your reality is made possible by the shifting of energy. The shifting of this energy is created by consciously or subconsciously focusing your vibrational offerings into a place where the conscious vibrations of the whole experience will respond and co-create with you.

When you remember and review your past, you are consciously focusing your energy vibrations into an offering that maintains those memories and has the potential to manifest the same activities in your present or future experience. Therefore, you must learn to control your memories. Remember, there are no actual lines of definition between your past, present, and future energy offerings. Therefore, they all flow together to create activities of the now and the future. The life force of God always travels on the forefront of this flow. The forefront of that flow is where you consciously control the vibrational energy that you are offering in a playful and creative way.

When you observe activities unfolding in front of you, you are focusing energy. When you plan something, you are focusing energy. When you organize something, you are focusing energy. When you project your thoughts, you are focusing energy. When you connect with your emotional feelings, you are creating focused energy. When you give or receive, you are focusing your vibrational energy. When you love something, you are focusing some of the higher vibrational energy you have. When you are touching, listening to, viewing, tasting, or smelling something, you are focusing your vibrational energy offerings, and the list goes on and on. Then, when you bring in the focused energy vibrations of your imagination, your desires, and your intentions into the equation, it multiplies the potential many times over.

The key to creating the vibrational energy that you choose to offer to the co-creation process is to know that it takes focus and to know that you can do this very consciously with powerful intentions. Then, know that the universe absolutely will respond to the vibrational energy you are offering for the co-creation experience that you desire.

By consciously controlling the many aspects of your focus, you will create all that you desire by shifting energy from the imagination to your reality, from your desires to the physical experience.

Ex.

1. *List all the ways you can focus energy. (Use all that we have shared and add many more to the list.)*
2. *Then write out three ways in which you can control each of these avenues of focus. Examples: love, kindness, patience, persistence, more energy, more effort, etc.*

Knowing the ways in which you control your focus or your vibrational offerings will improve your connection with the manifestation process.

97..... What are the things that you should be excited about while you are here? Obviously, the opportunity to love and be connected to God's presence are on the top of the list. The physical expression of life also tops the chart. What you must remember is that billions of souls have come before you and created many unique ways of living and being. Each and every one of those souls were inspired from within. They did not need to know what they should be excited about and inspired by. They knew what they were inspired by through their connection to God and that carried them to all corners of the earth while performing all manner of heroic activities to uplift the greater soul within.

The source of your guidance with inspiration and excitement will always flow from God while being transformed within your Greater Soul and then flow into your soul flame where it creates your reality. **Knowing what you should be excited about and inspired by is a simple process of accepting the flow.** Assume that you are a live puppet at the same time you are the puppet master and the master of the puppet master. Your guidance and inspiration does not truly come from one place because it is a flow that comes from all aspects of God.

Every aspect of God flows in and out of every other aspect of God. So, when we speak of the source, we speak of that portion of the source that is within you and flowing through you in combination with that portion of you that you know is present in all things. In other words, the presence of God within you guides the presence of God within all; at the same time, the presence of God in all things guides the presence of God within you. So, the things that you are excited about are the things that God is excited about.

98..... **For all souls there is a great desire to be challenged.** This desire flows from you at all times to the degree that you are inspired by the vibrational signals being sent from God. God is the source of your desire for challenge that creates growth. In order to grow, your greater soul and your soul flame will pursue the challenges that you desire. Without being challenged mentally, physically, emotionally, and spiritually, all aspects of God known today would not exist.

God is continuously spreading seeds of desire that attract challenge in your life. Those seeds are small but powerful bundles of energy full of life waiting to become active. As you receive these units of desire, you begin to nourish these desires by making them your own. Your greater soul recognizes them and creatively forms them into a more personal aspect of your soul. From the mixing bowl, they flow to your soul flame collecting similar vibrations from the universe as they move through the resonating coils that feed your soul flame with the creative life force. The activities that unfold in your physical world at the point of creation are the creative challenges which you and God have designed. **Activity and personal growth explode out into the universe as each challenge enhances who and what your soul desires to become.**

You must keep in mind that the challenges you are privileged to encounter are of your own co-creative design in the full presence of God. You must recognize that every aspect of your spiritual growth is connected to all that takes place in your life. You must know in your soul that life is a fantastic gift of your own co-creative design pieced together by one challenge after another.

Ex.

1. *Imagine a challenge facing you.*

2. *Imagine all the possible ways in which you might experience growth from this challenge.*

3. *Make a note of those growth experiences you would most desire and ask God for them to be present when the challenge unfolds in your life.*

4. *Thank God for the challenges which create growth in your life.*

5. *Feel the excitement of life flowing from the challenges you face now and the excitement of those which are waiting for you in your future.*

If you are excited and thankful for the challenges your soul will face in this lifetime, you will meet them with enthusiasm. Like a bowling ball knocking over the pins, nothing will stand in your way because you are on a roll. You are on a lifelong roll because you are looking forward to meeting your challenges head on in order to reach a high scoring game that you can be proud of. **When your challenges become your target, you have the upper hand, and life becomes more exciting.**

Ex.

With every challenge that you recognize in your life, take a deep breath full of excitement and speak the words, "I'm on a roll," as you release the breath and unleash your desire to attack the challenge.

99..... Every soul is a leader or a follower at different points in their life. In fact, you can be both a leader and a follower in the very same moment. If you recognize all aspects of who you are then you are always the leader and the follower in every moment. One of the beauties of our dualistic way of thinking is that opposites attract. These opposites overlap in each experience to make a unique blend of activity in our lives.

Remember that each of your life experiences does not start and finish at a well-defined place, because time is one continuous experience. Just because you start a stop watch and end a stop watch does not mean that you have captured or controlled time and the flow of energy from point A to point B. **Every event, whether it is timed or not, has lifetimes of energy flowing into and out of it.** You cannot even define a point in time so precisely that it does not have nano electric vibrational energy connected to the front and back side of that activity or portion of time. **Things take place in all directions at all times so there is no way to completely define the only direction of flow, let alone the true beginning or end of that event.**

Opposites attract because of the vibrations that are being offered. When you think about a leader and a follower at separate times, separate images are created in your mind of what these are. When you imagine a leader, you will always imagine a follower as part of the equation? Because you have given energy vibrations to these definitions as one experience, the law of attraction ties these two opposites together as one bundle of energy.

Backward and forward are the same energy vibrations because they were imagined in your thoughts as two aspects of one process. In and out, right and wrong, plus and minus, give and receive, positive and negative, are all opposites that carry the same vibration because they define the same process. **If you were to define the beginning of a circle, at that point you would also be defining the end of the circle, and the vibrations that are created at that point are the same. Opposites attract because they are the beginning and end of the circle.**

On the other hand, if you compare right and wrong, to give and receive, the thought vibrations are quite different. They are still connected in the truth that all things are connected, but these vibrations attract quite different things because they are in different circles.

So, when we are focused on attracting the vibrations of leadership to a situation in our life experience, we must also know that followers are attracted by the same vibrations. One supports the other and vise-versa.

If you can remember that you are all aspects of the one experience, then you will view yourself as both the follower and the leader and, of course, it will be so. In order to connect with and learn more about one aspect of any duality, you must learn to focus on the aspect that you desire. Focus does not separate the resonate vibrations of any duality, but it does create a point of view. When your point of view defines you as a leader of an activity, then you are most definitely the leader. If your view defines you as the follower, then you most definitely are the follower. If your view fluctuates, then you are both leader and follower.

Your focus is the key to your point of view, and your point of view is your experience. If you are experiencing God as being the leader, then God is also experiencing being the follower in that same moment because God is all aspects of being.

100..... Desires are in a state of constant change, as all things in your soul are. **Recognizing your new desires and reinforcing them is a very important ongoing process in your life.** It is a process that keeps you in touch with your greater soul. It allows you to be connected with the most important part of your data base, which is the addition of new material and how it connects to your previous desires.

Your soul flame is like a book being read and interpreted. Each page that you turn holds new meaning to who you are becoming and what your new desires are. Enthusiasm for each page that you turn comes like a mystery story that fully engages the creative thinker within you. As you are receiving the story, you are writing the story and manifesting it in the physical world.

Ex. I.

1. *Write a statement about something you feel internally.*

2. *Without pausing, add a statement of how you desire to feel.*

3. *Write three or more of these statements in the same manner as the examples that follow.*

> ➤ *I feel unhappy and I desire to feel joyous.*

or

> ➤ *I feel happy and I desire much more happiness.*

> ➤ *I feel deceived and I desire to feel loved and honored.*

or

> ➤ *I feel loved and I desire much more love and honor from my family and friends.*

> ➤ *I feel weak and I desire to feel much stronger.*

or

> ➤ *I feel strong and I desire/deserve to feel my strength on a much higher level.*

4. *Read the statements you have created out loud to a friend or to your angels, guides, and God.*

5. *Ask yourself if these statements are 100% true? If so, thank God for uncovering your true feelings and desires.*

6. *Speak the words, **"I expect my new desires to be expressed and followed from the depths of my heart and soul. And so it shall be."***

It does not matter what the starting point is (positive or negative). It is the truth of the statement that you are feeling that is important. Finding the truth in your desires will keep you connected to your changing desires. It does not matter what you desire to feel as long as it is the truth of what your greater soul is in desire of.

How you desire to feel is the recognition and reinforcement of your new desires.

Ex. II

1. Using the statements from exercise I, separate the statements of how you desire to feel from the portion that is how you currently feel. (Use only the statements of how you desire to feel.)

2. Speak them 21 times while thinking about them intensely along with imagining them as being your new reality. This will reinforce them to the point where you can already feel the more positive and productive vibrations that you desire and deserve.

3. Know that God is already responding to these new vibrations and they are being supported in your life now.

Repeat exercises I and II once a week if you choose to stay closely connected to your new desires as your life changes and unfolds.

Note: The process of stepping away from our past desires and into our new desires takes place naturally in each soul flame as we live our life, but using these exercises to intentionally pursue our new desires will propel us forward much quicker and more powerfully. If you are ready to move forward, then you must intentionally take the step that moves you forward.

101..... Imagine that you are floating in a large tank with more compartments than you will ever be able to count. The compartments are filled with vibrational energy. They are units of high quality vibrational fuel waiting to be used by you in order to manifest all of your desires. You simply need to know how to access them to release their powerful vibrations. It occurs to you that your body also contains billions of energy vibrations waiting to be used in the same manner as these in the tank surrounding you. So you gather your highest and most powerful thought vibrations and release them into the compartments of the tank. You find that as you release higher vibrations into your surroundings, the compartments of the tank respond by matching and releasing these same vibrations and much, much more. The vibrational energy within the whole tank raises to levels in which the manifestation of your desires are easily created. This same process does go on in the cells of your body and mind.

Vibrational fuel tanks are located in all things, living or non-living. All souls or gatherings of souls and larger units of God contain higher vibrations waiting to respond to the co-creation process. Their fuel feeds the flames of all God's desires as in those of your own soul. **The release of your higher vibrations always stimulates the higher vibration in all things around you.** Even the higher vibrations created by a beautiful mountain view will stimulate the bodies, minds, and souls of all that view it. Acts of love and kindness, thoughts of spiritual growth, and joyous activities all stimulate the release of higher vibrations in our physical and non-physical environment.

The universe is created and held together by the bonds of resonating energy that flow between all things. Whether you are responding to the vibrations around you or in the process of creating them, you are always responsible for the vibrations going on around you. Alignment with your surroundings and who you truly are is very important to what you are creating and becoming.

It is not always simple to stay in alignment with higher vibrations when the vibrational cukka-poo around you hits the fan, but it can be done through your desires, intentions, dedication, and spiritual practice. For thousands of years, monks have done it through meditation, prayer, chanting, singing, and spiritual practices. If you are to control your spiritual path and the environment around you, you must also use these techniques and others that work best for your own soul. To access the true nature of God in your life, you must pursue higher vibrations through spiritual practice, and it should be your highest priority at times when your soul's desire is to grow in awareness. **Surround your life with higher vibrations and your life will be ridiculously full of love, happiness, and creative inspiration.**

102..... There is always a better feeling and a more optimistic view awaiting you. There is always more love to be experienced on levels of awareness you only dream of. What you seek grasshopper extends far beyond the boundaries of your present awareness. There will never be a lid on the levels of God's love available to you. The more you search for a higher loving feeling within your soul, the more you will find it. The more optimistic you are the more optimistic you become. **The more you love God the more of God you will find to love.**

There is no reason that God would limit any aspect of herself to any degree. There are many great souls leading the way into the highest levels of awareness. Your path will never follow exactly in the same path as others, but we can assure you that you will reach these same levels and greater as you follow your own path into the depths of God's love. Your path is so unique and exciting that many great souls are watching and participating in your growth as a means to expand their own awareness. This is a technique that you also use extensively from the awareness of your own greater soul. At times your greater soul's energy flows into the experience of many soul flames in the same way that our energy is now flowing through the soul flame of Makenneth Stoffer to participate in a larger shared experience.

Because your experience inspires our growth and our experience inspires your growth, the communion of this one experience becomes so grand that it is a challenge to comprehend, but this great challenge is what we seek. **All souls are seeking the union of oneness through the communion of God.** The web of God's love is immense and that is a very simple understatement at best. **The most important thing to remember is to be happy with who and what you are and be excited about where you are going.**

So rejoice in the future of all, because it is a spectacular one on every level of awareness. We will always be traveling together because it is one community of souls and one co-creation event. Even your term the big bang does not do justice to the reality of what we are becoming. It is more like a big bang, ba, ba, ba, ba, bangitty, bang, bang, bang to infinity and beyond.

103..... **If you can reach your destination emotionally, then you can also reach it physically, mentally, and spiritually.** We are defining emotions as gatherings of information formed from the mixing and combining of many units of feelings bundled together as one powerful unit. So it surely makes sense that if you are to grasp the reality of your new desires, then you must connect emotionally in order to understand them. Once you have a handle on them emotionally, you can start to piece together the mental and spiritual aspects that will bring them into existence in the physical experience.

The flow of emotional energy in the mixing bowl of your greater soul is like a whirlpool of God's love and deepest feelings stirring in the belly of your soul. When it comes together and settles out, your creative future is in alignment with God's desires and yours. When your soul flame allows the emotional connection to be made with your greater soul, your path becomes clear, and it unfolds in perfect alignment with the desires of your greater soul and all that God desires through you.

Again, if you can reach your destination emotionally, then you can also reach it physically, mentally, and spiritually.

Ex.

1. *Imagine a physical destination on your path.*
2. *Imagine the spiritual destination that coincides with it.*

3. *By imagining the physical and spiritual destination, you have already reached the mental and emotional aspect of the destination. Solidify this emotional destination by describing how it feels in completion.*

4. *Remember that emotional bonding is what creates all of your destinations in life. Thank God for your ability to emotionally bond with your future.*

104..... Desire flows through all things and is created from within all aspects of God. **Desires are the urge for new possibilities in the continuous growth of God. To feel your desires coming forth is to feel life flowing from your soul.** When you are in a state of free flowing desire, there is no lack. Desire leaves lack behind when it ventures out to create new pathways. Life is not founded on or created by lack in any way. **Life is created by desires that always manifest abundance to the degree of your conviction to them.** What is your present conviction to your desires?

All that is taking place in your life is a manifestation of your desires, and you are the controller of these desires. These desires are neither good nor bad unless you label them as such. Do not be afraid of your desires or the labels that others may place upon them. They are your desires meant to serve the creation of your life, not the creation of other lives. If your desires are held back in order to serve the lives of every other soul, few of your desires would manifest. There is a reason your desires come to you, and you are meant to pursue them. The Holy Spirit has chosen to express desires through you. **From your point of view and your point of creation, your desires are perfect for your experience at this time.**

For God to be infinite in her expansion, her desires must be infinite. This means that all desires will be experienced and re-experienced in all souls as they move through this sea of co-creation.

Your portion of the co-creation experience is to pursue the desires that you know are true for your own path. This means they come from being in alignment with God and are not held back from the true path that you have chosen.

If you want to take one step forward, slap your wrists and say, "oh, bad desire, bad desire," then retreat back; this is the experience that will be your path. It is much more productive to find your true desires and pursue them by being in alignment with the desires of God. If there are times when your desires don't feel good then you must readjust your alignment with them. Desires that don't feel good are a sign that your desires are not pure. Pure desires will always produce an outcome that feels good. Adjusting your desires is an ongoing process in your life, and it is always done through the co-creation process.

Ex.

1. *Write three or more desires that you have at this time in your life.*
2. *Imagine these desires being completed in your life.*
3. *Imagine how it feels to have them completed.*
4. *Rate how good you feel about their manifestation. Choose a number one through three, with three being pure satisfaction and the greatest feeling you can imagine.*
5. *If some of your ratings are less than three, answer the question, what would make me feel better about the manifestation of this desire?*
6. *Re-adjust the wording of your desires and the projected outcome, then rate how good you feel once more.*

7. *Once your feelings of manifestation match your projected desires, you will know that they are pure desires.*

8. *Return to this list of desires in a week or a month and see if your feelings are still true, then readjust them as needed.*

9. *If you return to this list of desires and they have truly manifested completely in your life, pat yourself on the back and again ask the question, how good do I feel about it? Even after manifestation of your desires, you must readjust your desires to include more aspects of them as they relate to the life ahead of you.*

105..... How do you truly know if your present physical experience is the best possible path for your greater soul? Remember that your path is created by the desires of your greater soul. So, if your soul flame is burning bright that means that you are in alignment with your greater soul's desires. **If your life feels good, then you are in alignment with your greater soul and your soul flame is burning brightly.** If you are allowing the wisdom and love of your greater soul to flow fully into your soul flame, you can be sure that your soul flame is burning brightly and your present physical experience is on the best possible path. It is possible to monitor the abundance that you are creating in all areas of your life in order to know whether you are truly pursuing your purest desires that would indicate that your path is the best possible path for your greater soul.

You can start by monitoring the desires that are about to manifest in your future.

Ex.

1. *List your desires and the manifestation that you expect to take place from these desires.*

2. *Then ask the question, do I feel like these desires and the probable manifestation are the next logical step in my life? (Answer the question truthfully and from your heart.)*

3. *If your desires feel unreachable then they are not close to manifestation, and you may or may not be on your best possible path. If this is so, then you should redefine your desires. If you feel that your desires will be manifest or you know that they will manifest as they are the next logical step in your life, then you are on the best possible path.*

This three step process will help you monitor your path by keeping realistic desires. Realistic desires are the largest part of your best possible path for your greater soul.

106..... Your body holds many vibrational energies. They are stored in all areas of the brain, the heart, the liver, the blood, your bones, etc. These energies have been created by the activities of your life, your thoughts, your emotions, your spiritual expression, and the interaction of the environment on your body.

The vibrational memories of your entire life are stored within the cells of your body. Memories that you bring forth from past life times can also be stored in the body. Even your daydreams and your creative imagination are stored within.

The purpose of storing these energies is for access to them if you so desire. In the same way that memories are accessed, you can also access the vibrational energies that accompany them. Access to these vibrational energies come through the emotional body which is deeply integrated in all aspects of your body. Mental and spiritual vibrations are always flowing through your body, stimulating the emotional vibrations that are held within your emotional body.

You may have noticed that many of your love centered vibrations are stored within your heart, creating the radiance of your heart chakra. Your throat chakra holds many vibrations related to communication. Your crown chakra holds vibrations related to spiritual wisdom.

Storing and using vibrational energy from within the emotional body is a normal process in all living things. What you store and what you access in your emotional body is determined by your interpretation of the events of your life. Remember, you are in control of the way in which you interpret every aspect of your life.

God, your greater soul, and your soul flame are always part of the process when creating, storing, and accessing the vibrational energy within your emotional body. Making peace with your internal, emotional vibrations is very healthy for the physical body and mind and is a powerful way to access the healing process.

Ex.

1. *Access any issue from your past that has been stored in your emotional body. Do this by pulling up an old memory.*

96

2. *How did your interpretation of the situation create the emotional vibrations, and where do you believe they were stored in your body?*

3. *What positive thoughts and feelings can you add to the memory in order to change it? Access as much gratitude as you can. Your positive re-interpretation of this past event will be stored in the same place where you originally retrieved it. The more you engage in this re-interpretation process, the higher your internal vibrations will be and the healthier your body, mind, and soul will become.*

4. *Thank God for allowing this positive re-interpretation process and thank your body, mind, soul, and emotional body for accepting it.*

107….. If you simply follow the same routines, you will re-create the same patterns in your life, leaving little room for the expansion of your awareness. **You must learn to offer new and higher vibrations to the universe in order to receive new and higher vibrations from the universe.** If you desire to create higher vibrations, you must release the past and look forward to creating something new. You must think, feel, imagine, and do it in order to create it. Everything that comes to you is in response to this process of creating it. Creating it is the way in which you invite it and allow it into your life.

Creating it from your desires is the way in which you cut this new path to higher awareness. You certainly know that you have cut every aspect of your path up to this point in time; why would it be any different from this point on? So go forth and create it.

Use the inspiration flowing from the Holy Spirit to creatively cut a new and better path to higher awareness. The question is, are you ready, willing, and is this your time to move on to a much greater vision of your place in this universe?

Are you ready to think, feel, imagine, and do what it takes to co-create your highest spiritual awareness?

Ex.

1. *In silent meditation for the next 15 minutes, imagine what it is like to be in the full and complete presence of God.*
2. *Feel the powerful energy vibration you have just created within your soul.*
3. *Feel the Holy Spirit flowing through all things.*

4. *Answer the question, what is God's love guiding me to pursue, at this time, in order to raise my souls vibrations to the next level?*

5. *Think, feel, imagine, and do all that it takes to follow this path to the next highest level.*

108..... Prayers, in their simplest form, are communication with God. Because prayers take place in the present moment, they will always effect the energy vibrations in the future. That energy is usually strongest in the moments of the prayer and shortly after, but the effects of the prayer continue to manifest throughout your lifetime and beyond.

The strongest elements of any prayer are thankfulness, appreciation, gratitude, and love. If you include all of these elements in a joyful expression to the universe, the Holy Spirit will flow into your soul and every aspect of your life. When your life is overflowing with this presence, your vibrational energy can be guided to create all of your desires.

Prayers open your greater soul to receive more of Gods loving vibrations. **Prayers notify the universe of your desires by creating a resonate vibration that attracts the activities which your soul is desiring to manifest.** That is why prayers make things happen in your life.

Prayers of thankfulness, appreciation, gratitude, and love for the activities of your past carry into the future and create a joyful path to follow. Those same prayers with focus on future events have the same joyful effects. If you start your prayers with gratitude for the past and carry them into your desires for the future, you will create the strongest bond possible in your communication with God.

> *Prayers of gratitude attract vibrations of gratitude.*
> *Prayers of thankfulness attract thankfulness.*
> *Prayers of appreciation attract appreciation.*
> *Prayers of joyfulness attract joyfulness.*
> *Prayers of love attract vibrations of love.*
> *God's answer is always in the response to vibrations that match what you are radiating.*

Ex.

1. *For the next 21 days practice writing a new prayer every morning or evening that includes all four elements (thankfulness, appreciation, gratitude, and love). Write this prayer so that it connects with your past and carries into your desires for the future. Make*

sure that joyfulness is expressed as you are writing each prayer.

2. *Read the prayer over and over until you feel every element of the prayer flowing from your soul.*

3. *Expect all of your desires to be known and manifest by the power of this clear communication you now have with God.*

Writing and expressing your prayers in this way for 21 days will create a most wonderful form of communication with God that you will use for many lifetimes to come.

109..... **Everything you do in life is a focusing of energy.** The question is, how effective is your focus? How effectively are you controlling your manifestation process with your focus? Do you recognize and understand all the things in your life that requires focus? If your attention is on it then you are focusing on it and creating something in your life. Learning to guide your focus through your intentions is a very powerful way to control your life. Self-awareness of what you are focusing on is very important because random focus may create something that you do not truly desire. For example, you may randomly stare at attractive breasts of the women around you and attract a slap in the face if you are not careful. If you desire something other than a slap in the face, you must focus with intention. This intentional focus may lead into a focused conversation and much, much more.

Use the exercise that follows to grasp a better understanding of what things you normally focus on. Once you are aware of all the things you focus on, you can begin to focus on these things with intentions to create what you desire.

Ex.

1. *Review the list (Items of Focus) that follows, then go back over it and assign a value to each type of focus. **Which ones do you believe will be most powerful in your life for creating the things you choose to manifest?** Use a scale of 1 to 7 with 7 being the highest.*

2. *Assign another value of 1 to 7 based on those you believe that you use the most in your daily activities.*

3. *Add the two values for each item together and review the list again to see which items have the highest combined values. These are the focus items that you are creating the majority of your life from.*

4. *Go over the list one more time and identify the items which you should or could use more often in order to increase your power of focus and therefore your power to manifest what you desire.*

5. *Which items from the list will you learn to control by intentionally focusing on them when you need to?*

(Items of Focus) List

Pondering something

Touching something

Feeling something emotionally

Listening to others

Listening to your environment

Viewing things

Walking somewhere

Smelling things

Making/building something

Teaching others

Giving/receiving something

Loving something

Imagining something

Remembering something

Observing something

Projecting something

Organizing something

Planning something

Changing something

Redoing something

Meditating on something

Praying about something

Desiring something

Daydreaming of something

Holding something

Caring about something

Being happy about something

(Feel free to add to this list)

After finishing this exercise, are you somewhat amazed at the amount of focus that you use throughout the day to manifest what you desire? Is it possible now for you to believe that everything in your life is a product of the desires that you focus on? Do you recognize how much control you have over the focus that you project in order to create the world around you? **Are you willing to intentionally focus on the things that you desire?**

The resonating vibrations that you create everyday by focusing on your desires, attract these same vibrations from every direction in the universe. This attraction is how the universe supports the manifestation of everything that you focus on. The fact that you have been intentionally focusing on the wisdom and self-awareness techniques in this book has inspired you and allowed you to create a whole new aspect of yourself. This is just the tip of the iceberg, to what you will be creating of your own greater soul in the infinite progression of becoming a greater portion of Gods awareness.

A Fun Prayer/Affirmation

Wow, Wow, Wow, Wow, Wow, Wow, Wow, Wow!

Wow, Wow, Wow; Z, Wow, Wow, Wowl-Zir!

Wow-------Wow-------Wow!

God loves me! Life is Awesome!

110….. The fact that vibrational energies attract each other in this universe is the reason larger and larger forms of life come together to create something new. Attraction among vibrational energy is a growth technique. **Energy loves to combine and grow; that is why the universe is expanding wildly. The sea of God that we live in does not just flow together; it grows together.** The sea of God is the light that consumes the darkness through growth. The nothingness that the physical and spiritual universe expands into becomes the light of God. Attraction, bonding, and re-bonding is what allows the universal energy to flow. Creation of new energies from the source are flowing everywhere into the universe as needed or desired. God's intentional focus is immense.

When you, as a physical and spiritual being, connect and bond with other living energies or the environment around you, you are partaking in the vibration of attraction that creates this universe and allows it to flow freely with new life. You are a very important part of the creation process. You are the creator. **At the place where you create is the place where God expands as you.**

111..... You must be consciously aware of the vibrational range of energy that you are working with and, more importantly, the ever expanding aspect of this range of energy. The reason there is a range of energy vibrations that you are working with is because your greater soul has created it on this level within your soul flame based on the desires that it has for expressing itself at this time. This range of vibrational energy is very functional for you at this time, but will always be expanded as your life carries on.

The reason there is no limit to the vibrational energy that you can experience is so that the greater soul can expand your range of vibrations as needed in order to experience more of God through you. The progression of this expansion within your soul flame is in unison with the desires of God and your greater soul. **Remember this whole process is about God's desire to experience more of God's own being in every creative way possible.**

The more consciously aware that you become of your range of vibrations and your desire to expand this range, the more God's desire is to provide the expansion of your vibrational range. Therefore, expansion becomes your reality simply because you are the co-creator of your own reality.

So how do you become more consciously aware of your vibrational energy range and the expansion of it? There are many elements to this equation with an infinite number of pathways to follow. We would like to suggest that you make a desire filled decision to become more consciously aware, then follow up this decision by using the personal awareness and spiritual practices in this book. Use those practices that call out to you based on your soul's desires. Spiritual practice creates the higher vibrations that you need in order to become more conscious of who and what you are in relation to where you are going on your infinite path of growth. Practice makes perfect and this perfection allows greater awareness of who and what you are becoming.

Conscious awareness of your vibrational range and the expansion of it is a simple decision to be made in every moment of your life. An ongoing decision to be more conscious of your new awareness will be one of the greatest and most loving paths of your life.

Ex.

1. *Through silent meditation, focus on your decision to become more consciously aware of your vibrational energy range. (15 minutes)*
2. *Allow powerful vibrations to settle in to your soul flame while expanding your aura with breath work. (5 minutes)*
3. *Feel grateful for your opportunity to become more and radiate this gratefulness to all things. (5 minutes)*

112..... **Good thoughts and good feelings are the easiest to have and maintain.** They are also the easiest to bring into focus and manifest, either intentionally or unintentionally. Good thoughts are the most likely to produce a physical outcome because they are supported most by your greater soul's desire and the desires of God. Good thoughts are the most common and the most highly supported form of higher vibrational energy. This makes them very predictable and controllable. Good, kind, and loving thoughts are the stability of our universe. Maintaining good, kind, and loving thoughts will produce the most amount of satisfaction in your life.

The satisfaction that comes from thinking good thoughts is one of the biggest parts of manifesting physical things in your life. Satisfaction is the desired inspiration that creates all major aspects of growth in your expanding awareness. All souls are tuned into this aspect of personal and spiritual growth. Through the satisfaction of energy being well used and well spent, more good thoughts and feelings arise.

Because your soul knows the power of good, kind, and loving thoughts, they will always be produced in order to enhance your life. You will produce them easily and at will.

Ex.

1. *Imagine and produce a good, kind, and loving thought about someone or something in your environment.*
2. *Allow all of God's presence to flow into this thought and the feelings that accompany it.*
3. *Know that God's presence is working to produce a physical, mental, and spiritual expression of your thought, both within you and within all aspects of your souls environment that are the object of your focus.*

4. *Be thankful and grateful for the outcome of all your good, kind, and loving thoughts.*

5. *Feel the satisfaction of your soul as it knows that it has just created a better place for all souls to gather in the presence of God. (It has raised the vibration of your environment and in turn has created satisfaction in all things.)*

113..... One of the best ways to control your process of manifestation is to create kind and loving thoughts attached to your desires. If you are desiring the expression of sex in your life and you attach kind and loving thoughts to your image of it, then you will produce a deep spiritual experience with it when the activity takes place.

If you attach kind and loving feelings to your experience of driving before you head out to work, then your experience will be meaningful and safe as you drive to work.

If you pause in your moment of hatred towards the actions unfolding around you and attach kind, loving thoughts, and feelings to it, you will control the events of your life.

As a conscious intuitive being, you will be able to imagine the coming events or pause within them and attach kind, loving thoughts, and feelings. **A powerful soul such as yourself can and should be inspired to control your life with the simple choice to express love and kindness in every event of your life.**

Attaching loving thoughts and feelings to the most important events of your life will always create higher vibrations than the event would have produced without your input, interpretation, and control.

You truly do have the power to control every aspect of your perception of the events of your life and influence the perception of others. Attaching kind and loving vibrations to the events of your life will inspire others to do the same.

If you do not like the outcome of a certain event, even after you attached kind and loving energy vibrations to it, then you surely would not have wanted to be there if you would not have done so.

We can assure you that every event in your life is better with a little sugar on top, mostly because that means that you are controlling your own destiny in a way that aligns with your soul's desires.

Ex.

1. *Create any imaginary event you can think of. Whether you label it good or bad does not matter. (It is interesting that you can label an event good or bad even if they may never take place.)*

2. *Imagine kind loving thoughts and feelings attached to this imaginary event, then allow yourself to re-experience it in your imagination.*

3. *Which imaginary event do you have more attachment to? The first or second one?*

   Note: There is a reason everyone loves a movie with a happy ending; they desire to remember it more than others and desire to watch it over and over. ***Love is the prevailing force in all of Gods activities, real or imagined.***

114..... It is not what you say, it's what you feel when you say it that resonates with source. **The way that you feel about each aspect of your life is the vibration that you are resonating with.**

This feeling is your declaration of what you desire to attract at your point of creation. Your feelings cause a magnetic attraction which collects these same vibrations from the universe and builds your reality by what you focus your desire on. Being conscious of your desires and feelings is how you focus and control what you are creating in your life. If you focus your feelings on wealth, then that is what you will create. If you focus your feelings on the lack of wealth, that is what you will create.

To create feelings of wealth that will attract wealth, keep two or three hundred dollars in your wallet in order to know that you can buy the things that you need or desire. Each time you think about what you could buy, you are creating a feeling of financial abundance. If you do not spend this money, yet allow the vibration of financial abundance to be with you for weeks or months, you will attract many vibrations of being wealthy from the universe. As long as you do not negate these feeling of abundance with self-talk about lack of wealth, you will soon create much more wealth in your life because you have focused on your positive feelings of wealth. Create the feelings and they will come. They, being the manifestations, which you desire.

This process of creating financial wealth can also be used in the same way to create spiritual wealth. As long as you create the feelings of spiritual abundance from your desires, you will be focusing on the manifestation of your spiritual path, and it will be created. **If you are in tune with your feelings, you will know what is about to manifest in your life.** The more focus you put into your desires through your feelings about them, the more in tune you will be with what you are creating. Knowing the timing of your pending manifestation can be very important because it will help you organize new desires. As your desires manifest, it is wise to transfer the momentum of your creative process into a new or related desire. In this way, you can manifest one thing after another. The creator must continue his love of creating. The more he creates, the more he is inspired to create, and it's all done through how he feels about his desires.

115..... What is the voice in your head? Do not place limitations on what you believe the voice in your head is. Because you have a vast expansion of spiritual family, well connected throughout this universe, your voice can be heard by many and also becomes the voice of many. **The voice in your head is never just one voice, and yet, it is always the voice of one.**

As Makenneth Stoffer hears what is one voice in his head, he also knows that this voice comes from the voices of many wisdom counsel leaders and dedicated participants. This includes many groups or networks of voices being sung from faraway places in this universe, and they make up the full spectrum of God's voice.

Every soul has this type of network available to them, and yes, every soul does use it as needed and desired. Every soul is channeling the voices of many into one voice that they believe is that of their own mind. In reality, it is the one voice of our one mind. Most of the time in your life, you are hearing the one mind so clearly that there is no separation in the voices that come together to make one powerful voice, and other times you will recognize individual voices.

Your soul will always create its identity in the combination of group interactions that it desires to be part of. The Greater Soul is a unit attached to a much larger unit which is attached to a much larger network of units. Therefore, the web of God's mind and soul is what you are. **Your identity crosses over into all aspects of the one mind, the one voice, the one soul, the one being, and, of course, the one source of all life.**

Many times you choose not to follow the voice in your head because your soul has an agenda, and it knows or believes that the message is unclear or not in alignment with the creative path that your soul desires.

The voice in your head can be as disjointed as the clutter of many confused souls, or it can be as clear and powerful as the complete voice of God. You must use the power of your initiative mind to know what is the most productive source of information. **If it feels good and feels right as related to your soul's desires, then it must be your true path, no matter what the outcome is.** The outcome of events do not determine the path desired by your greater soul. It is the experience your soul desires.

If you focus on what feels right, feels healthy, and productive, then you will be hearing the clarity of God's voice and connecting with the clarity of her mind and soul.

If it feels healthy and productive, then it will feel right, and if it feels like the next logical step, then it is the voice of your angels guiding you. When you feel that the voice in your head is in perfect alignment with the next logical step of your life, you should thank your guides and the larger spiritual network that you

117

are connected to, because they are inspiring the will of God within you.

116….. If you have opened up a fortune cookie recently, you may have noticed that fortunes are on the way out and positive inspiration is in. Inspiring affirmations are perfect for the fortune cookie because they actually inspire your desires and affirm positive ideas that will truly help you create your future. **Affirmations are a proactive way to create your fortune** instead of believing a random magical experience will be bestowed upon you by the grace of God.

The source of this next exercise came from a fortune cookie that I received after a fine buffet. The inspirational fortune read –

"Do not let what you cannot do interfere with what you can do".

Ex.

1. *Based on your skills and talents list all of the **things you can do** to make things better for:*
   a. Your health
   b. Your family
   c. Your friends

      d. Your community

      e. Your home

      f. Your country

      g. Your spiritual growth

      h. Your awareness

      i. The planet

      j. The future of mankind

2. *For each statement of what you can do, write a statement of how you would go about doing it and what the possible outcome would be.*
3. *Go over the list again and underline the "can do" activities that you believe you should start right now in order to improve your life and the lives of those around you.*
4. *Think about all the things you can and should do, then pray for guidance to achieve them at the appropriate time in your life.*

When you have a list of all the things you can do, and you are pursuing them, you will have no time to think about the things that you cannot do. The things that you cannot do will have very little importance while you are in the process of pursuing the things that you can do. When you are ready, the universe will bring forth many new talents, and there will be new things that you can add to your "can do" list. Your lifetime can easily be filled with the things that you can do. If every person pursued his can do list and expanded it as he goes, the world would be incredibly healthy, happy, and productive. If you desire to make your mark in this world, you should enthusiastically pursue your can do list and your work will be known to many.

The can do list we choose to create in this section was focused on what you can do to make things better for yourself and others. If you desire, there are many other areas of focus which you could use to be more specific to specialized areas of your life. A sport or game that you love, a job or career path, a hobby, a specific relationship, a spiritual pursuit, or a dream of yours. There are many areas of your life that can be dramatically improved by increasing your awareness of what you can do. You should also help your children create "can do" lists. Teaching them to work with what they can do will give them a life-long technique that they will praise you for long after you have passed and, most likely, they will teach it to their children and grandchildren. In fact, many of the personal growth techniques in this book should be taught to future generations of your family and the community if you have higher aspirations for the future of mankind.

There are many souls among us that do have higher aspirations for the future of mankind and the future of all souls developing in every aspect of this universe. We joyously welcome you to this brotherhood of souls. It is your true family, and it will continue to grow as the Holy Spirit expands infinitely into the greater awareness of love.

117..... Every soul is connected to the source. The soul receiver is always full and always processing the feelings and thought vibrations that God source is providing. It is impossible to exist without this inflow. It would be like a cell from your body being separated from its source of nourishment on every level and set aside to die. The reality is there is no desire on the part of the soul or the whole to set a portion of itself aside. In fact, there is no place that this can be done. Separation from the whole would only be an illusion. Therefore, when you feel separate from the source, you are actively engaging in this illusion. You are simply not allowing enough of the source to flow in, which creates a sense of uneasiness in your soul as feelings of negativity. At this point, the vibrations that you are offering to the universe are less than what your soul desires, and less than the Holy Spirit desires.

121

Restriction of the flow is always a matter of being self-imposed and must be changed by the true desires of the soul. Understanding the vibrations you are allowing into your soul receiver and the vibrations you are offering to the universe are a complex aspect of your personal growth.

The best way to know where you are at is to listen to your own feelings. Reconnecting to God on a deeper level is always your best option. Prayer, meditation, breath work, and focused intentions are among the most powerful forms of reconnection to source. Dedication to these practices will reconnect you to your desires and enhance the flow of God source through your being. Every thought and feeling that you entertain will then move you closer to your connection with God source.

118..... Ex.

1. Buy the best quality pillow case that you can find and visit a shop that laser prints photos and designs on cloth.

2. On one side of your pillow case imprint the phrase "**I care**" and on the other side of the pillow case print the phrase "**I love.**"

3. Every night at bedtime place the side up on your pillow that your soul chooses. Think about the people, places,

and things you care about or the people, places, and things you love.

4. *When you wake up in the morning and see your pillow, follow the same process you did at bedtime of thinking about what you love and care about.*

5. *Don't hesitate to carry your pillow to a place on your couch where you love to curl up and cuddle up with the things you love and care about.*

It is time to wake up and care about all the things you love in your life on a much higher level than you have ever experienced before. If you can wake up and care about all that is going on in your life and the world around you, there is no reason that we, your spiritual family, should not consider you as the true saint that you are.

As you wake up and care about all that is going on around you, you will soon make a habit of allowing these feelings to change the physical world around you. As this takes place, not only will you know that you are truly a saint, but those in your life that love you dearly will also proclaim that you are a saint to them and this world. As you follow this path, the Holy Spirit will always be with you.

119..... There are vast numbers of souls in this universe, with each and every one of them quite different. Each soul is unique in the vibrations it maintains and in its desires. The patterns of creativity that each soul constructs are as special as each perfectly unique snowflake. Because we all have different desires, we will never completely understand the intricacies of each soul's path. Even those individuals with desires that match our own vibrations perfectly are working from a different point of view, different level of awareness, and in a uniquely different body, mind, and soul.

It is not easy to grasp the fact that everything we see, feel, hear, or sense in any way is uniquely different from us, yet still part of us. Because our desires are always different, it is important to remember that we will never fully understand the desires of our fellow soul mates. So when it comes to laws, rules, guidelines, suggestions, teachings, and any form of guidance, there is no soul outside of yours that can completely clear the path that your soul desires. You should follow the creative path of another soul only if it does not interfere with your own desires. Exploring a similar path is great fun and can teach us many things if we remember to follow our soul's desires as we go. You must remember that different paths of each and every soul combine in order to make the one path, and, on this one path, all rules suggestions, guidelines, laws, and teachings are only temporary until they can be expanded, changed, and improved based on greater awareness.

We are not suggesting that you go against every rule that is unjust or not in alignment with your soul's desired path. We are suggesting that you work within the rules long enough to change them, or change your circumstances of bondage attached to them. **Learning from and breaking away from guidelines and teachings that do not serve your desired path are the ways in which your soul grows and expands.** You must choose your path wisely in order to accomplish all that you are here to enjoy.

Do not worry yourself over rules and regulations if your soul's desire leads you with the internal guidance of the Holy Spirit to a different path. If you follow your heart and **the golden rule, (do not intentionally harm others and your environment),** then you will be travelling the path of your soul's desire and the true path of God.

Studying the components of your soul's desire and your core beliefs will help you choose the direction of your path. The presence of the Holy Spirit in every aspect of your being will always guide you. Listen to your guides and angels, but most of all, listen to the voice of God within.

The universe cherishes the uniqueness of every soul and the creative paths they choose. If it were not this way then all that you pursue would not be provided. The nature of this infinitely expanding universe is very simple. **In each and every moment, you and all that you experience must be unlimited in order to make the free choices that come from your unique point of view.**

120..... The golden rule, (do not intentionally harm others and your environment), can sometimes be tricky business. At times you may find yourself in the presence of a circumstance that calls for a decision that clearly cannot be avoided, and the outcome will cause harm to one or more parties. A win-win alternative should always be creatively pursued, but there are times when the only win-win situation is the lesser of two evils. In this type of situation, much prayer and internal guidance must be pursued to determine the greatest good for all. You will have much guidance

126

on all levels when faced with the greatest decisions and challenges of your life. You will never find yourself in any situation without the guidance of God. Turn inward with love in your heart, and your decisions will always be made clear.

The golden rule will keep you on the high road and steer you home when you are lost or when you think the whole world has lost its way. For all souls within the physical body, the golden rule will be broken every day that you consume nourishment from plants, animals, and other living energy sources. To be alive in this physical world, you must partake in the consumption and transformation of physical energy. It is important to remember that even as we gain nourishment from the death of living things, there will never be a true death to the spiritual energy within all things. Because there is never any real harm to the spiritual energy of every soul, you may question the purpose of the golden rule, and we would say that respect for the sacredness of the physical body is very important because it allows each soul to grow.

The purpose of living a life with the highest ideal of not intentionally harming others and the environment is to create a harmonious, stable environment in which each soul is recognized as the perfect reflection of God. Every part of the whole must be treated with kindness and respect. You must remember, as each soul creates itself, you are an integral part of that creation. **Every single activity that takes place in this universe is you, with no separation between you and God.** To connect with every aspect of yourself and your activities, you must take time each day to watch the activities of others around you. Then speak the words, "wow, that's me; hitting that home run, holding that child, crying for help, shooting that gun, laughing with friends, playing on the merry-go-round, etc."

Not all of what you see taking place as part of you will you like or dislike, but still it is part of you and you must ask yourself, why am I doing this? How can I do it better? What healthy vibrations can I create and maintain in order to support all that I desire to become?

It is not wise to cut off thy own hand because it does the work of God through those that I do not understand. It is much wiser to live by the golden rule in order to understand my own ways and recognize my reflection as the true reflection of all things.

121..... If your focus and attention are on the way things are, then your experience will be held to the way things are. This may be fine for a portion of your life, but it will be holding back the flow of what you are becoming through this limitless growth experience.

God is always ready to expand the divine awareness within your being. When you are ready and willing to become more, there will be nothing holding you back. You will always notify the presence of God that you are ready to expand your awareness by your intention to pursue growth. This intention is expressed by your soul's desire to hold your attention on something greater than the way things are. **If you always know that there is something greater than the way things are, then you will discover what God is guiding you towards.** God's greatest love is to expand your awareness. Love, happiness, kindness, and all that you do are enhanced by each step forward in your awareness.

You can only know your truth from the place where you are at right now. The exciting part is there will never be an end to where you are at right now. To be fully present within your own truth means that you are living in the absolute truth of your present awareness and that your attention is focused on the pursuit of much greater things to come.

The seeds of greater awareness are already planted; you just need to let them grow from the nourishment of your soul's desire in the fertile garden of the Holy Spirit.

122..... If you want things to change to a higher and healthier vibration, then you must pursue those vibrations in the places that you desire them. Pursue them in your heart, in your head, in your body, in your house, in your family, in the community, in your car, at your job, at dinner time, while praying, while meditating, while holding your child, while playing in the woods or anywhere under the sun, etc., etc. You need to define the places that you will be pursuing higher vibrations. Notifying yourself and the universe that you will be pursuing higher thoughts, feelings and actions in these specific places will open the door and clear a space for your own will to manifest. If you imagine it, create it from your heart and soul at the place in your environment where you desire it, the universe will match your desires at this same place.

Your intentions to pursue higher vibrations within everything you do is the key to experiencing these higher vibrations everywhere that you go. The more you focus your intentions on higher vibrations, the more powerful they become. You will always be the generator of those vibrations that you choose to use in order to enhance your experience.

123..... While placing your attention on the desires of your soul, you must support this process with the projections of all relevant vibrations that will create the manifestation you have imagined and intend to allow. You must set aside all labels and projections that you have created that do not serve your soul's desire. This includes labels that you have projected upon others and those that they have projected upon you. You must set aside past experiences that you have projected on others and they have projected on you. You must create your future from the pureness of God source. The creative force flowing through your soul is the source of all relevant vibrations. **Allow the vibrations that inspire you most to guide your decisions on which relevant vibrations you will be projecting in order to create your desired outcome.** Imagine that God source is a color pallet in front of you. Your soul is the paint brush and your life is the canvas to be painted on. Mixing these colorful vibrations on your brush is the work of the creator within you, and your soul's desire will creatively guide the brush as it splashes color into your life to create a picture that tells a story to all. As in an art museum, the story of your life is viewed and creatively interpreted by many viewers based on their own experience and point of view. Your job is to create the art work. The creative interpretation of your life is exciting to many, but it is not relevant to the deeper connection you have with God who created the masterpiece in the first place.

124..... Every soul in the body of God has a desire to make a difference or, in other words, support and creatively expand the awareness of God. **Your first and most important role in the expansion of this great sea of oneness is to know thy self by pursuing unlimited growth within your own soul.** The opportunity to pursue your personal growth has never been better than it is at this place and time because now is the cutting edge for all of your future growth. On the cutting edge, you will always express your strongest desires and set them in motion. God has created your soul so that you can enhance the awareness of God. **Again, your first responsibility is to creatively enhance your own awareness at the point of God's awareness that is you.**

As you attend to the desires of your soul, you will find that one of your strongest desires is to support the desires of other souls, especially those that you feel very connected with. Because so many souls on every level of awareness support all that you are, there is a natural flow of this loving energy which will always spill over into the souls you are connected with. In other words, there is no escaping the shower of love in this universe because you are sitting in the middle of the tub with many souls splashing and playing together in order to create all aspects of the infinite being and every soul's desire to make a difference in known by all.

125..... As you live your life, there are lots of vibrational activities going on around you. You do not desire to be a part of many of them. You cannot change the vibrations that others create; you can only choose to include them or not include them in your life. We ignore many thousands of undesirable vibrations every day. Most are easy to ignore simply because we cannot attend to all of them, so we choose those that seem pertinent to our life. We tend to focus on those that take place in our circle of friends and family. Even within our circle, we block out those we do not feel connected with. We do not respond to statements that are made by others if they are not directed towards us, and many times we do not respond to statements that are directed at us. If verbal statements or activities are in sync with the vibrations we are putting out, then we respond with enthusiasm.

One of your most important goals to remember should be not to be drawn into the vibrations of others if they are not aligned with your soul's desire. How many times have you walked away from a conversation that does not interest you at a party or gathering? You must remember that you are always in control of your life and all the vibrations happening around you. You control them by the attention you give to them. Analyzing your view point on each vibrational activity is the best way to sort through them. If you desire to, you can change your own perception of any activity around you by matching it to your own vibrations. By creating a viewpoint that is in sync with your core beliefs, you will control your life.

Maintaining the thought vibrations or feelings that you desire are a very powerful way of attracting only those vibrations that you choose to be a part of. Maintaining and expanding your thought vibrations and feelings in life is not an easy task, but it is the way in which you create your life.

Prayer and meditation combined with your intentions to follow a path of higher vibration will always help you maintain your pursuit of relevant vibrations. **If you're following your soul's desire, your**

soul will always be happy, satisfied, and at peace with the path that you have chosen.

You will maintain your creative freedom, not by controlling the behavior and desires of others, but by maintaining or adjusting the vibrations that you are projecting and receiving.

126..... The universe as you know it, is that all things equal a vibrational frequency, or, in most cases, a very complex structure of vibrational frequencies. These frequencies can be maintained for short periods of time or long periods of time. In fact, time itself is a frequency that is maintained in order to create many things in the awareness of God. The physical universe with all of its planets, stars, and galaxies are also a frequency that is held in order for all to grow and expand in this unique medium. Every frequency, whether it is held for a short or long duration, is very powerful in that it creates new things. Thoughts and feelings are so flexible and creative that their vibrations can create anything imaginable. Thoughts and feelings always create something bigger through the infinite combination of them.

This is why we speak so often of the law of attraction, which is our thoughts or feelings attracting the same frequency in order to create all that we desire. **We resonate with the frequencies that**

creatively express our desires. There is no frequency that will not be answered by that same frequency; therefore, the perception of lack can only be experienced if you attract it. Abundance is created in the same manner. Your hand is always on the frequency dial and your potential to create is unlimited. Time is of no real significance; therefore, you may create your desires now, later in life, in the next lifetime, or in many to come. **If the frequency is held, you will co-create your desires.**

127….. Consider the cactus or succulent plant and its ability to propagate. If you remove a handful of its segments and place them in the soil, new plants grow from each spot if the conditions are right. The questions is, would this truly be a new plant or is it the same DNA, spirit, and consciousness now growing in different places in your yard or your mom's yard hundreds of miles away? The plant may have many new perspectives on life now, but it is all still one aspect of God growing in many places and it does have a shared intelligence. In this same way, many other plants drop portions of themselves as seeds in order to manifest themselves in new places. Just because one portion of the original plant or animal has completed a growth period and fades away does not mean that its conscious perspective of that place and time is lost.

136

It simply transfers through its DNA to many places, hundreds, thousands or millions of years into the future. The consciousness of all living things is transferred in a similar process of continuation. The Holy Spirit is also continued and expanded in this same way. The spiritual energy of this universe is no different than the physical world, in that it also grows and expands into much greater things of which you will always be a part of. Therefore, what you are now is an important part of what you will be in the future. Because all things come from one source, it is very simple to see that you are in all things. **When you recognize that you are in all things, it is much easier to remember that you love all things.** It is this love that expresses who and what we are as one perfectly creative flowing spiritual awareness.

128..... Why is it that we are faced with so many decisions here in the physical world? Does life on the other side have the same amount of decisions facing each soul?

In the physical world, you are faced with the constant movement of dense matter in order to maintain your being. The density of the physical realm forces you to make one decision after another because life can only be maintained through the movement of your body. At every moment, you and your body must make choices in order to live.

In the vibrational field of energy that you maintain on the spiritual realm, things are much more fluid. Therefore, maintaining your vibrational energy pattern is almost effortless. In spirit, decisions that you are faced with arise from the activity of your mind. There is no stress of making a wrong decision that will terminate your life or dramatically alter it in the way that the physical world can. So decisions are less dramatic and formed from within your own creative awareness.

Because decisions are much more dramatic on the physical plane of existence, many souls on the other side are highly motivated to participate in the activities of the physical world. Not only are they watching the show unfold, they are also participating in the guidance of all individuals on your planet and many other planets. Most souls have one foot in the physical world and one foot in the spiritual. If you remember that every physical being has the greater portion of their soul on the other side, you will realize how vested the spiritual realm is in the proceedings on the physical plane of existence. Therefore, your greater soul is always a very big part of the decisions made in your life.

138

Decisions are the spice of life which allow creativity to flow limitlessly in the physical world, yet, at the same time, your decisions can temporarily block the flow of creativity in your life. You should cherish the fact that decisions allow creativity and the opportunity to experience growth. If you are overwhelmed by too many decisions, simply make the decision to live a simple life that will reduce both the amount of decisions and reduce the possible stress that excessive decisions can create in your energy field.

Decisions are so much a part of your way of life that you can absolutely choose to live or die at any moment. "To be or not to be" is the ultimate power of God that you carry within you. To have this power and know that you have it is one example of evidence that you are the activity of God and that you can choose to make decisions that are ultimately from the strength, wisdom, and love of God.

Ex.

1. *Take a walk for a half-hour or more in a highly active area in a place with many people.*
2. *Focus all of your attention on watching the decisions made by others and your own self.*

3. With each decision you see and recognize, speak or think the phrase, "God created that decision."

4. When you take time to pause from this task of monitoring God's decisions, contemplate the overall orchestra of God's decisions and ask yourself, what is my connection to all of this? How do I feel about it?

5. Contemplate how important it is for you to do your part in making healthy, loving, life supporting decisions.

129..... Self-talk is a powerful tool for solidifying your aspirations. Self-talk usually promotes the vision that you desire. **In visualizing what you are verbally describing, you draw it closer to you.** Sometimes, you can almost touch it and you surely can feel the emotions of it along with the vibrations of its probable outcome. You can know any activity more intimately through your self-talk, visions, and dreams of it.

The pleasures of any activity in your life start long before they take place in reality. Also, the pleasures of it extend well behind the event into your memories. When you get good at connecting intimately with your future, you can learn to imagine the possibilities of the event and feel them as strong as they will ever be. This is a simple activity which you can perform through your imagination to guide all of your experiences.

Self-talk will create that intimate desire you have for a specific activity in your life. **When the intimacy is created, the activity is already in the process of manifesting.** Imagination, visualization, and self-talk are the prelude to every event in your life.

Learn to perform the following exercise consistently, and you will talk yourself into all manner of activities that your soul desires.

Ex.

1. *Think about a few things you believe you will do in the future because you desire to do them. Then enter these visualizations into the phrases that are provided below. Describe the same visualization in each phrase. Then redo the process with a different visualization that you desire.*

2. *Answer the following questions while your imagination constructs images of what you are self-talking about.*

   a. I believe it will be really exciting when I

   _____.

141

b. I know I will feel great when I

_____.

c. I am sure my life will be awesome when I

_____.

d. I am determined to

_____.

e. God will support me when I

_____.

3. *After you have intimately described your desires, visions, and plans for the future, ask yourself what your confidence level is regarding the possibilities of achieving them.*

4. *Repeat the process every day for 7 days then ask yourself how important your dreams and desires are? Again, ask yourself about your confidence level to see if you are sure you are going to achieve your desired visions.*

5. *Decide how important your dreams are and ask yourself whether your self-talk conversations need to be continued. If so, expand by adding more details every day until the desired outcome is 99.9% probable.*

The more intimate you get with your desires for the future, through self-talk and envisioning them, the more you will enjoy the process of manifesting your dreams and the actual physical event. The important events of our life must be savored. **The greatest impact of any event in your life will come from the intimate connection you build with it while you are putting the effort into acquiring it.** Like a day at the beach, you don't sprint out on the beach and acquire the warmth of the sun in 5 seconds and then return to your car to go home. Taking time to feel the warmth and beauty of what you desire is very important. Therefore, most souls will savor and remember the entire process because some events take a lifetime to unfold. When you go to the beach, stay for the sunset and beyond because life is worth savoring.

130..... When I speak, do I speak the word of God? This is a question you must know the answer to at all times. At all times the answer is, "ABSOLUTELY."

You must not forget this truth because it is your guide to knowing that you speak the word of God through your own unique and powerful voice. It is also what guides you to choose your words wisely in order to improve your life and the lives of those that you love. God has no desire to speak harsh words through your voice in order to harm others emotionally. Therefore, each of your words are chosen wisely to enhance the love of God expressing through you.

Please remember that you are the love of God in action and your words will create this love. To speak the word of God is wise, but to know that you speak the word of God is truly a gift from within. **You have the ability to praise and give thanks to God in every word that you speak.** The words that you speak will soon create your reality. Therefore, you should always create your reality with the words that give thanks to God. This is why you must speak the truth as you know it from your heart.

You will notice that as you speak, you are creating your own reality and your own identity in the same breath that you are expressing the love of God. You are inseparable from God in the words that you speak; therefore, you should respect and even cherish the words of every soul who speaks in the voice of God.

God's word has been given so that you will create with it, and so it is that you do create with it. When you begin to know the power of what you create with your words, you will recognize the power of God within you. Knowing yourself as this power is a true blessing and your divine birth right.

144

Ex.

Sing this mantra for 7 minutes or more to enhance the power of God's voice through your words.

The words I speak create my life,

God's words are mine, God's words are mine.

The words I speak express my love,

The power within is mine, the power within is mine.

The words I speak soothe my soul,

God's words are mine, God's words are mine.

When this mantra settles into your soul, the way you speak will forever enhance your connection to the Holy Spirit within you.

131..... Every desire that you have is experienced on at least four levels. The level that you are most familiar with is the level which has direct attachment to physical outcomes in your life. You feel your desires coming from within, and you proceed to manifest them. The outcome of your desires is the satisfaction that you have created what you need.

The second level of desire comes from a place within your greater soul where emotional connection is the underlying goal. Because the physical experience is only a vehicle for the collection of soul experiences, level one is the creation of your needs, and this activity of creation transfers the emotional connection of this interaction back to the greater soul which is level two.

Level three involves the emotional, mental, and spiritual energy that you have created being shared with a larger portion of God. For example, the many souls gathered together within the wisdom counsel or many other larger expressions of God.

Level four, being the whole experience, is obviously the complete experience of your desires in the co-creation process involving every aspect of God.

So you can see how important every phase of the God experience is and how your desires affect all of it. You can also see that co-creation has many levels to be considered, some which we have not spoken of and many more which are yet to be created in the expanded awareness of God. Just to keep your mind open a little, how do you believe your desires interact with the universe of sub-atomic life deeper with you? Life is everywhere and so are your desires present in all things. If your desires were not present on all levels, you would not create anything and you would not be anything.

Thank God, that through your desires you are all things.

132..... Your life can be self-monitored through a progress chart of your own design if you choose to measure your progress in specific areas of your life. For some souls, the order created by a progress chart can be very inspiring, motivating, and highly focused.

Consider the motivation towards productive activity that the merit badge system provides for the Boy Scout organization. Then just for fun, imagine that your society was a little more advanced and used this productive merit badge system to retrain the criminal populations. Then imagine that your government institutions could be revitalized and more productive by using a similar merit badge system.
Then imagine that educational and spiritual institutions could

greatly enhance the personal growth of their members through a merit badge system.

Structured growth, inspired by your greater soul and the presence of God is what we are describing through recognition and praise. This does not mean that creativity is sacrificed. In fact, the greater the platform of structured growth, the greater the productive activities will flow from it. **From greater structure, the opportunity for greater creativity is provided and inspired.**

Even in the spiritual realm, we do provide ceremonies for those who have achieved greater levels of awareness. The ceremonies serve the same purpose as a merit badge. Recognition of accomplishment is a resource that we use to inspire personal and spiritual growth. Personal and spiritual growth benefit the expanding awareness of God on every level; therefore, we encourage you to engage in the personal progress chart that follows.

Ex.

List all the areas of personal growth that you would like to monitor. Use some of the following and create those that are most important to you.

The Personal Progress Chart (Example)

Personal Growth Items	*Day 1*	*Day 2*	*Day 3*
1. Spiritual practices	2	1	etc.
2. Prayer	1		
3. Meditation		1	
4. Happiness expressed	3	2	
5. Self-control		1	
6. Feeling of satisfaction	2	1	
7. Kindness expressed	4	2	
8. Feeling loved	2	2	
9. Love shared	2	1	
10. Connecting with others	2	3	
11. Community support		1	
12. Physical health pursuit	1		
13. Uplifting others	1	1	
14. Feeling your desires	2	1	
15. Feeling good	3	1	
16. Expressing yourself	2	1	
17. Laughter	1	3	
18. Singing		1	
19. Chanting	1		

20. Recognizing God	*3*	*1*
Today's total:	*32*	*24*
Personal Happiness Rating	*10*	*8* *(1 – 10)*

This chart is to monitor your life and inspire more growth. After marking your chart with the number of items initiated each day, look it over at the end of every day, add the total, and give yourself an overall personal happiness rating of 1 to 10. The happiness rating is not based on the totals, but how you feel about what you have accomplished.

Looking at the personal happiness ratings over time in correlation with the totals of each day, you may discover that some personal and spiritual practices may have a more positive influence on your life. Pursue these items more intensely if you so desire to create higher levels of happiness and satisfaction in your life.

133..... The more you create and maintain good feelings in all that you do, the higher the vibrational frequencies you will maintain, and in turn, attract more of these same vibrations into your life. There are many ways to maintain good feelings in your soul, mind, and body. Exercise, good food, exciting activities, accomplishments, singing, chanting, playing, meditating, praying, laughing, smiling, etc. It is the creative combination of these things that really makes you feel good day in and day out. But, there is one that you can use at will and always raise your vibrations to a feel good level above all that you are doing.

This mental activity is appreciation. Appreciation can be created at will, by focusing on an aspect of God and feeling love for this person, place, object, or idea. Appreciation is created through mental focus and opening of the heart center to accept more of God's love into your vibrational pattern. The more you practice appreciation, the more you create it. The intention to accept more love is how you create the good feelings of appreciation. Appreciation is not carried out in order to prove that you love a certain aspect of God. It is done to make you feel good and raise your vibrations to a higher level. Anytime you accept more of God into your heart and soul, you are raising your vibrations. Appreciation is all about making you feel good. You don't even have to share it with anyone other than God in order to feel good because sharing it with God is sharing your appreciation with all.

Appreciation is one of the best ways for you to create good feelings because appreciation is created at will, and in that same moment it also creates more love, kindness, happiness, acceptance, and many other powerful vibrations. **Appreciation bundles together many good feelings and allows you to internalize them on a powerful emotional level.** As you reach a level of awareness where appreciation for all things becomes a constant flow of higher vibrations, you will also reach a place where good feelings and feeling good are never separate from your precious experience of life.

Every moment of your life is about appreciating the constant flow of God's good feelings moving through your being. Appreciation always raises the level of God's vibrations in you at least one step above the awareness you would have without it. It's time to take one step up in your life with the appreciation that creates higher vibrations and allows you to feel good about all things in your future.

You can rise above by utilizing the steady flow of good feelings which come from appreciating the love of God in all things.

Ex.

Create a habit of appreciative self-talk. For the next 21 days, ask and answer these questions throughout your day as often as you can during your normal daily activities.

1. *What is beautiful around me?*
2. *What do I see that I appreciate around me now?*
3. *What is happening around me that I love?*
4. *What am I grateful for right now?*
5. *What should I be grateful for in my future?*

As you ask and answer these questions often and randomly, you will create the habit of doing so. The habit is what we are after. So, if you get stuck on just one of these questions and repeat it all day that is great.

134..... In what ways should I be communicating with God?

a. Conversations with all aspects of God.

b. Self-discovery exercises that engage in feeling the presence of God.

c. Self-discovery exercises that engage in knowing the presence of God.

d. Self-discovery exercises that engage in being the presence of God.

One of the very best ways in life to start a meaningful conversation with any soul is to ask questions. Questions that explore life's possibilities always demand the interaction that will provide the wisdom that is being sought. **If a question inspires a conversation between two or more aspects of God, then a meaningful conversation with God is underway.**

If you can inspire a conversation with God between a few souls, then why not inspire the same conversation with God on higher levels by including many souls on many planes of existence? Why not include God on the highest level by intentionally asking the whole expression of God to be present for your conversations.

The truth is, every question you ask inspires a powerful conversation on all of these levels. In your process of conversing with God, you must learn to recognize the deeper aspects of communicating with the source.

Learning to feel the conversation and feel the presence of God in every aspect of the communication you have is one of the higher virtues of learning to be fully present and activated within every conversation.

Knowing that you are in conversation with God is also one of the most important aspects of the conversation. You cannot be fully present in any conversation if you do not know that you are fully present. Know thy self and you will know God.

In order to engage in your deepest conversations with God, you must feel, know, and be the presence of God in all things.

Ex.

> *Hold your hands over your heart with your eyes closed and feel the presence of God. Then know that God is radiating from your heart to the entire Universe. Then be the presence of God radiating throughout the Universe. You are now in communication with God. Take a deep breath and release it slowly as you ask a question and allow the communication to flow.*

135..... There are two types of vibrational energy in the creative process of your life. The first is instantaneous or primary expression. This process is not bound by the constraints of time until the phase where your soul flame transfers its vibrational energy into physical expression as your body and the activities of your body, which you know as the expression of life. This secondary expression is the vibrational energy which is constrained by time and space.

Primary expression is everything that takes place within; the source, the greater soul, and the body of God which manifest instantly. All thoughts and feelings manifest vibrational energy instantaneously and are from primary source. For example, the feeling or thought of love instantly creates that love.

Kindness, joyfulness, happiness, excitement, passion, pleasure, pain, confusion, emotions, and much, much more are created instantly through your intensions to do so. This is the way of the spiritual realm as primary expression. You know instantly when you think a loving thought that you feel that loving vibration throughout all things. Therefore, if you ever feel like you desire more love, you simply think and feel it instantaneously into existence within your vibrational expression. **Primary expression is instantaneous manifestation of the Holy Spirit.**

Because your soul flame is expressing itself within a physical body that moves throughout the physical world, a secondary vibrational expression which you sometimes refer to as the real world, manifests under the constraints of time and space. Energy movement under the constraints of time and space allow primary expression to experience density, which is the physical world that you are functioning in.

Secondary expression then includes the process of manifesting activities in the real world. Time is an elaborate illusion that allows our primary expressions to be dissected and played out in a very unique, step-by-step expression of life. Time is a medium that allows a very diverse perspective on who and what we are as the experience of God.

Manifesting your will as the will of God in this intensely slow or dense medium of time can be very frustrating and very challenging. This challenge is why we came here; it is your greatest opportunity for personal growth. It is a place to learn, grow, and joyfully play. **Secondary expression is mostly about exploring happiness and the deeper levels of love that God has chosen to become.**

Transferring your primary expression into the secondary expression for your life is a little bit like a science experiment. This experiment has many outcomes which you have chosen to experience. When this lifelong experiment is concluded, your soul will have grown immensely and provided your greater soul with a beautiful gem to be cherished throughout all of eternity.

No matter how you view the intense experiences that you encounter from within the experiment, they are all greatly understood, appreciated, and cherished by the greater soul as your secondary expression returns to its primary state.

136..... *Heart Warming Exercise.*

> *1. Relax, be comfortable and tune out everything.*

> *2. Close your eyes, feel good and feel protected.*

> *3. Breathe gentle and slow as you feel the presence of love build up within you.*

> *4. Allow pure love to grow and radiate warmth from your heart.*

5. *Feel this warmth penetrating your body like the sun on a hot day and visualize a powerful circle of love forming around you to contain the warmth of your soul.*

6. *Warm your body in the light of your soul for 7 - 10 minutes, then imagine bringing one of your friends into the circle of warmth where they feel nothing but your heart's love.*

7. *Feel the bond between each of you as the warmth in both of your hearts creates a much larger umbrella of light radiating love to all things.*

8. *Bring others into the warmth of your heart and allow the circle of warmth to grow to great proportions.*

9. *Bring any person, place, thing, or idea into this great circle of warmth to increase your bond of love with it.*

10. *Bring all aspects of God into the circle of warmth and be grateful.*

11. *As you transition into the rest of your day, bring the warmth of your heart with you and warm the souls of all who you meet.*

This heart-warming exercise is a tool you can use to bond with all things in life. Use it to bond with all aspects of God on the deepest levels possible. Use it to create a peaceful, joyful, happy, and loving connection with all that life has to offer.

This spirit filled heartwarming exercise is one of the greatest tools that we use in the realm of pure spirit. It is a vibrational energy connection that we use to bond with all beings and all aspects of God on all levels of awareness. **Heartwarming absolutely creates more love in this Universe. It is a source of new energy in the vast experience before us.**

Your decision to engage in the heart warming practice is one that will greatly enhance the levels of vibrational energy you are working with, playing with, and exploring. We use it on the highest levels of awareness and encourage you to do this also. Can you imagine the changes that would take place on your planet if the leaders of your great countries, religious organizations, social groups, and businessmen would use the heart warming practice on a daily basis? Can you imagine if the members of your family and your friends used it daily?

Heart warming is a higher level of prayer, and you do know the powerful things that prayer has created in your life, on your planet, over your history of existence there. In your future, there will be many new forms of prayer because your connection with God is the most important aspect of your existence.

Made in the USA
Lexington, KY
05 June 2017